The Washington Ethnic Food Store Guide

Second Edition

Jim C. Lawson

Ardmore Publications
Washington, DC

Copyright 1992 by Jim C. Lawson

International standard book number: 0-9623888-7-4

Published by

Ardmore Publications
P.O. Box 21051
Washington DC 20009-0551
(202) 234-4859

Second Edition

To order a copy of *The Washington Ethnic Food Store Guide, The Baltimore Ethnic Food Store Guide,* or *The Washington Ethnic Bakery Book* by mail, send $9.95 plus $1.50 for shipping to the above address. Add 60¢ DC sales tax if applicable.

Table of Contents

Introduction

While keeping abreast of the ethnic markets scene since the first edition of this guide, I kept running into new markets and a few that I missed — and there were some that closed and some that changed their orientation from one group to another. So, I concluded that all you ethnic food enthusiasts out there needed an updated guide.

In this second edition you'll find stores for four additional groups — British, Laotian, Portuguese, and Russian — as well as more stores for the old groups.

Interesting phenomena have been the establishment of large ethnic supermarkets (Lotte, Lucky World, Korean Korner, Americana, Mount of Olives, Asian Village, and Kam Do) and expansion into more than one branch (Lotte, Lucky World, Americana — again).

Old groups with large increases have been the African category for which we have seen an increase from 1 to 9 markets, Middle Eastern from 9 to 20, Philippine from 4 to 9, Indo-Pakistani from 30 to 52, and Latin American from 29 to 48.

In any venture such as this, it is impossible to claim that every ethnic market in the metropolitan area has been included. If you find one that I have missed, please drop me a line at the publisher's address.

In the index you'll find listings by store name and by city. If you don't know a store's name, look in the listing for a city or town near you and browse the list until you find a store representing the ethnic group in which you are interested.

To make your store visits less stressful you should consider taking a cookbook with pictures and the dishes titled in the native language to the store. This can be a big help, if the store owners do not speak English very well.

For personal service, such as an explanation of how to cook something, go to the smaller stores which are more likely to be mom-and-pop operations and more capable of helping you. Large stores are good for exploratory shopping or if you already know, or can find out somewhere else, how to use a product.

Always call the store before your first visit. There is some degree of turnover in the stores, however it is much less than I anticipated. Hours and closed days can change, too.

For the serious ethnic food devotee, here are some books that have been invaluable to me in my encounters with all sorts of unfamiliar foods.

> **Bruce Cost's Asian Ingredients** by Bruce Cost, William Morrow & Co., 1988, $22.95.

> **Cook's Encyclopedia** by Tom Stobart, Harper & Row, 1980, out of print.

> **Cook's Ingredients,** The Reader's Digest Association, 1990, $14.95. Tells where the maze of ingredients found around the world originated, how they are produced, what nutritional values they have, and how they are prepared for the table. Photographs, but no recipes.

> **Cooking with Exotic Fruits and Vegetables** by Jane Grigson and Charlotte Knox, Henry Holt & Co., 1987, $17.95. Photographs, descriptions, recipes, and basic preparation techniques.

> **Encyclopedia of Asian Food & Cookery** by Jacki Passmore, Hearst Books, 1991, $25.00. 600 items described, 400 recipes from 16 Asian cuisines, including those of Nepal, India, Sri Lanka, and Pakistan.

Gastronomy of Italy by Anna Del Conte, Prentice Hall, 1987, $35.00.

Gastronomy of Spain & Portugal by Maite Manjón, Prentice Hall, 1990, $35.00.

International Wine and Food Society's Guide to Herbs, Spices and Flavorings, Tom Stobart, McGraw-Hill Book Co., 1970, out of print.

Traveler's Guide to the Food of Italy by Valentina Harris, Henry Holt & Co., 1988, out of print. Written for the tourist, but has good descriptions of the foods of the various regions of Italy.

Traveler's Guide to the Food of France by Glynn Christian, Henry Holt & Co., 1986, out of print.

Uncommon Fruits and Vegetables by Elizabeth Schneider, Harper & Row, 1990, $16.95. One of the best. Includes information on selection, storage, preparation, and usage, along with nutritional values. Recipes and photographs.

Von Welanetz Guide to Ethnic Ingredients by Diana and Paul Von Welanetz, Warner Books, 1987, $10.95. Descriptions, storage instructions, how to prepare and use, recipes, and list of ethnic cookbooks. Drawings.

Afghan

Afghan Market

5709 Edsall Road
Alexandria VA
703-212-9529

Daily 10 to 9
Parking available

Owner Azim Akram sells grocery products from India, Iran, Pakistan, and a few from Afghanistan (kishk or dried yogurt and mint leaves, for example). Afghan rugs, artifacts, books, videos, and music cassettes are also available. Expect to find Iranian breads (sangak, taftoon, and sweet saffron), herbs, and spices; Afghan nan and rogani; lavash; and pita bread. There are several types of beans, nuts, pickles, tea, flavored waters and syrups, and basmati and jasmine rice. The sugar-coated chickpeas and almonds make interesting party nibbles.

Afghan Mini-Mart

6566 Backlick Road
Springfield VA
703-455-7614

Monday-Friday 8 a.m. to 10 p.m.
Saturday-Sunday 10 to 10
Parking available

Along with standard American convenience store items, you'll find a few Afghan and west Asian products, including nuts, pickles, spices, herbs, dried beans, rice, and sweets.

Kabul Market

512B South Van Dorn Street
Alexandria VA
703-823-5213

Monday-Saturday 9 to 8:30 / Sunday 10 to 7
Parking available

Hafizullah Gawhary bought this market in the summer of 1991 and he sells halal chicken, beef, and lamb, in addition to groceries. Each August he brings in kharbuzeh grown in Arizona from Afghan seeds. These large melons (some reach 25 pounds) are sweet and crisp and reminiscent of honeydews.

Try the two Afghan restaurants a couple of doors away on either side of Kabul Market.

African
(South of the Sahara)

Buy African beverages such as palm wine, Ethiopian honey wine (tej), and Ethiopian and Kenyan beer in the Adams-Morgan area of Washington (18th Street and Columbia Road NW).

Indian Supermarket in downtown Silver Spring, Tu-Tu Market in Falls Church, and Washington's Acropolis have many Ethiopian products. West Indian and Latin American markets also sell West African products.

Addisu Gebeya

2202 18th Street NW
Washington DC
202-986-6013

Daily 9 a.m. to 10 p.m.
On-street parking

There were no Ethiopian markets in Washington for years and then within an 18-month period there are two — and just a few doors apart.

Addisu Gebeya, New Market in Amharic, opened in April, 1992, and sells a multitude of spices in quantities that will last the occasional cooker of Ethiopian food for many moons. Expect to see canned vegetables, grains, flours (including teff from Idaho), beans, German and Guatemalan honey, green coffee, incense, religious objects, wooden teeth-cleaning sticks, clothing, and a few craft items.

Try the snacks: qanta, or petite strips of spicy dried beef; dabo kolo, tiny pieces of fried dough (how do they get them in that unusual shape?); and kolo, a roasted grain and nut mixture.

Bruk's International Foods

6339 New Hampshire Avenue
Takoma Park MD
301-270-5937

Monday 10 to 8 / Tuesday-Thursday 9 to 8
Friday-Saturday 8 a.m. to 9 p.m. / Sunday 9 to 5
Parking available

Large and amply stocked, Bruk's is the star of Washington's West African markets. After a visit here, novices will want to rush out and buy an African cookbook. Meat and fish are the show-pieces. You'll see smoked and fresh cow foot, smoked and fresh goat, and stewing hens. The fish case displays some 20 intriguing kinds of smoked fish, including swordfish, oysters, grouper, and mudfish. Giant yams come from Ghana — smaller ones from Brazil. Shito, a Ghanaian hot pepper sauce flavored with dried shrimp, onions, and ginger is made in the United States and is served as a dipping sauce with kenkey or baked plantain. Kenkey, a firm, fermented cornmeal mush, is made locally. Yam and plantain flours, the basis of fufu, are also sold. The comprehensive spice shelf has products from Nigeria and the West Indies.

Take home a few chewing sticks, especially selected to aid in cleaning teeth and massaging the gums.

Eko Food Store

6507 Annapolis Road
Landover Hills MD
301-341-5050

Monday-Friday 9 to 9 / Saturday-Sunday 9 to 6
Parking available

Look for plenty of goat meat (with and without skin), oxtail, gigantic cow's feet, more diminutive pig's feet, dried and frozen fish, and stewing chickens.

Effie's Bakery in Alexandria provides two kinds of Ghanaian breads: a soft, lightly sweet loaf flavored with nutmeg and sugarless smaller loaves called Tea Bread, which are firmer and have a touch of spice added. From New York City come Jamaican hardo bread and spice buns.

Black-eyed peas, ground rice, gari, long-grain rice, and semolina are displayed in barrels. Fresh vegetables include tubers, coconuts, green and ripe plantains, and okra. Herbs and spices, both African and West Indian, are plentiful.

Don't overlook the prepared food section. There will be African and Jamaican patties and probably jollof rice; goat pepper soup; and moin moin, made with dried beans and lots of spices.

By the cash register you may see a small basket covered with a damp cloth. Inside are fresh kola nuts, which are savored widely in West Africa. Be warned, they are flavorless, but are mouth-puckeringly astringent. Shortly afterwards, though, you'll have a pleasant, clean taste.

International Foods

7611D Richmond Highway
Alexandria VA
703-768-1093

Monday-Saturday 9 to 8 / Sunday 9 to 5
Parking available

This West African-owned store is across the street from Mt. Vernon Square Shopping Center. In spotless new surroundings you'll find staple grocery products, a butcher section, and fresh produce for the cooking of West Africa, Latin America, and the West Indies.

Palm oil, egusi seeds, canned garden eggs (small green-skinned eggplants) from the west coast of Africa; from England come baked beans, salad cream, and vegetable salad by Heinz. Several items are from Jamaica and Trinidad, including an oyster cocktail sauce. The Latin American section is well stocked with canned goods, masa harina, beans, cookies, spice, herbs, and so forth.

Merkato Market

2116 18th Street NW
Washington DC
202-483-9499

Monday-Saturday 10 to 9 / Sunday 11 to 9
On-street parking

Tamiru Degefa opened Merkato Market in the fall of 1990 to the applause of ethnophiles who wondered why, with the 25,000 to 30,000 Ethiopians in the area and all the Ethiopian restaurants, we didn't have a market.

Like Indian cookery, the unique character of Ethiopian dishes is derived from zesty and savory spices, and lots of them. Well over half the products fall in this category and include fenugreek, anise, thyme, ajwain, cumin, caraway, ginger, garlic, coriander, mustard seed, white and black pepper, cayenne, whole and ground turmeric, and rosemary — and Ethiopian cardamom pods, which are about five times larger and have a more intense flavor than their smaller cousins. These are just the simple spices; Mr. Degefa puts together blends such as berbere, awaze, afrinj, and the mixture used to produce niter kibbe, or spiced butter. No room deodorant sprays are needed here. Open the door and inviting fragrances engulf you.

You'll also see green and roasted Ethiopian coffee beans, fresh meat, aenjera and ambaasha breads, dried whole and split fava bean from Egypt, rice, barley, whole and cracked wheat, split peas, dals, and chickpeas. There is also teff flour, the basic ingredient of aenjera and a healthy porridge.

Mr. Degefa has developed recipe sheets to hand out with several of his mixes. He will be happy to answer questions about his products, and even instruct you on making your own aenjera.

Middle Eastern products were added in 1992.

Yankari Grocery

645 Florida Avenue NW
Washington DC
202-234-4179

Monday-Saturday 9:30 to 9 / Sunday 12 to 4
Parking in rear / Near Howard University subway station

West African products include several kinds of dried fish; a good selection of spices and herbs; and powdered yam for fufu. From the West Indies come hot sauces and condiments, tamarind balls, and a fried-dough snack called chin-chin. Goat meat is sold, as are teeth-cleaning sticks and Nigerian newspapers.

Stop in at the interesting African clothing and craft store next door.

More African Markets

Al-Mac Food Imports

5922 Riggs Road
Hyattsville MD
301-559-0699

Daily 11 to 8
Parking available

International Food Store

6832 New Hampshire Ave.
Takoma Park MD
301-270-4470

Monday-Saturday 8 a.m.
to 9 p.m. / Sunday 9 to 8
Parking available

Oyingbo African Market

2431 Chillum Road
Hyattsville MD
301-277-3228

Daily 9 to 8:30
Parking available

British

The British Connection

119 South Royal Street
Alexandria VA
703-836-8181

Sunday-Wednesday 10 to 6
Thursday-Saturday 10 to 9
On-street parking

In early 1992, this store moved from its location on South Union Street and became a scaled-down adjunct of The Tea Cosy, a British-style tea room, which centerpieces such traditions as Scottish bridies, steak and kidney pie, bangers and mash, and the famous afternoon tea.

In the back room of the new establishment you'll find such products as orange barley water, chip shop-style mushy peas, Jaffa cakes, Weetabix cereal, salad cream, and gooseberries.

Cadbury and Mars (the English Mars) candies; English toffees; cookies by McVitie's, Mrs. Kippax, and Peek Freans; the popular Twiglets snack food; and lemon curd and other jams and marmalades by Robertson.

English teas (including PG Tips, Ty-phoo, and Fortnum & Mason); several ales (Newcastle Brown, Old Peculier, and Royal Oak are three favorites); and sweet or dry English cider.

While here, pick up information about joining the British & Commonwealth Society of North America.

Chadwick's

10 Annapolis Street
Annapolis MD
410-280-2748

Monday 1 to 5 / Tuesday-Saturday 10 to 5
On-street parking

Food occupies a small room in this emporium of products from the British Isles. Expect to see teas, jams, candy, biscuits, pudding mixes, Demarara sugar, syrups, and canned goods by the English Heinz company. In another section of the shop are several interesting British, Irish, and Scottish cookbooks, including some on such specialties as scones and proper teas.

Cambodian

Angkor Supermarket

937 University Boulevard East
Silver Spring MD
301-445-4174

Daily 8:30 to 8:30
Parking available

Angkor opened in the summer of 1990.   Here you'll find standard fare of Cambodia, Laos, Thailand, China, and Viet Nam. There are also fresh produce, frozen fish, and fresh meat. Try the Flower brand café au lait biscuits from Indonesia. Deliciously crunchy with coconut flavoring and a light glaze of café au lait, they make a wonderful accompaniment to a cup of tea. Ethnophiles are welcome and help is offered as soon as you enter the store.

Asian Grocery Market

4807 Columbia Pike
Arlington VA
703-892-5004

Daily 9:30 to 9
Parking available

Typical of Cambodian markets, this store has sizeable selections of:

Canned fruits: rambutan stuffed with pineapple, rambutan in syrup, jackfruit and toddy palm, longans, toddy palm seeds, lichees, banana in heavy syrup, soursop in syrup, loquats, carambola, mixed fruit, sugar cane, banana flowers, and sadao flowers.

Canned mushrooms: oyster, golden, button, straw, abalone.

Frozen whole fish: yellow catfish, milk fish, mud fish, pangasius fish, silver barb fish, spotted spiny eels, and climbing perch.

Fresh produce: green papaya, mints, lemon grass, coriander, mirliton, small round green eggplants, and fresh coconuts.

Oriental Super Food

4710 Columbia Pike
Arlington VA
703-920-0442

Monday-Friday 10 to 8 / Saturday-Sunday 9 to 8
Parking available

Even though this market is Cambodian-oriented, it has many products used in the Chinese, Lao, and Vietnamese cuisines. There are Cambodian newspapers printed in France and Canada and a large selection of rice.

Oriental Super Market

5001 Columbia Pike
Arlington VA
703-671-7091

Monday-Friday 9:30 to 8 / Saturday-Sunday 9 to 8
Parking available

Truly a supermarket, this store has good selections of all sorts of items from the Orient. Typically, fresh vegetables are a key feature of Asian markets and here you have quite a large selection including winged beans, long beans, banana blossoms, bitter melons, Chinese gourds, pomelos, guava, lemon grass, and herbs.

The meat department displays cuts of pork and fowl not normally found in mainstream supermarkets. There is also beef sausage made with rice, paprika, garlic, and galanga (looks like a ginger root, but has a flavor all its own); Chinese-style sausage (lap cheong); and packages of two small disks of nam (a pork sausage also containing rice, garlic, pepper, and sugar) with green and red chilies on top. Or, if you can find a way to prepare them, dried oysters, frozen apple snails, and miniature skewered and dried cat fish. In the beverage case are beers from Japan, China, Korea, and Thailand.

Chinese

Da Hsin Trading Company

811 Seventh Street NW
Washington DC
202-789-4020

Daily 9:30 to 7:30
On-street parking / Near Gallery Place subway station

Grocery products (limited to bottled, canned, and dried items) share space with gifts and medicinal herbs. I often find small ethnic stores such as this preferable to the larger supermarkets. Small stores are usually better equipped to provide advice on cooking and you don't have to stand in line to check out.

Da Hua Market

623 H Street NW
Washington DC
202-371-8888

Daily 10 to 8:30 / Thursday to 7:30
Parking in the rear / Near Gallery Place subway station

In Da Hua, the largest market in Washington's Chinatown, you can browse to your heart's content, reading labels and deciding on selections among several different versions of the same product. While rummaging through the vast frozen food section I discovered delicious, flaky shao bing — 2"x4" pieces of pocket bread topped with sesame seeds. On another visit I found spiced vinegar from the Philippines; it's made with fermented nipa (a palm) sap, fermented coconut water, onion, garlic, and loads of hot pepper, and is an assertive condiment, to say the least.

You'll see fresh produce; fresh meat, fowl, and fish; utensils; Asian vegetable seeds; Chinese wines; and a wide-ranging selection of Asian sodas and snack foods — shrimp-flavored chips and sweet potato chips are my favorite. Upstairs you'll find woks, utensils, dishes, gifts, and cookbooks.

Da Hua is the place to buy dried yuk chuk.

Heng Kang Company

730 Seventh Street NW
Washington DC
202-783-6030

Monday-Friday 9:30 to 8 / Saturday-Sunday 10 to 8
On-street parking / Near Gallery Place subway station

This is a grocery, gift, and herb shop. Its most interesting products are in the many apothecary jars — herbs and other products used in traditional Chinese medicine. How about a dried seahorse for your coffee table? Rubber soled kung-fu slippers are a steal at around $4.00.

Jack's Oriental Gift & Grocery

Sugarland Shopping Center
Route 7
Sterling VA
703-450-5141

Monday-Tuesday 11 to 7:30 / Wednesday-Saturday 10 to 7:30
Sunday 11 to 6
Parking available

Here you'll find a wide range of Asian food products with emphasis on Chinese foodstuffs. Owner Jack will advise non-Asians on how to use his products. He has copies of some 40 recipes to share with you. There are yam, halo-halo sundae, and mango ice creams; light soy sauce from Taiwan; Chinese and Thai cook books in English; and beer from Thailand, Japan, and the Peoples' Republic of China.

Kam Do Foods

4316 Markham Street
Annandale VA
703-941-8924

Monday-Saturday 10 to 8 / Sunday 10 to 7
Parking available

Edmund Tong's Kam Do (Golden Capital) started out in 1984 as a wholesale operation in Alexandria and, in the late eighties, added a retail section. In 1991, he moved his store into larger quarters in Annandale just off Little River Turnpike. For sale in this supermarket are products from China, Japan, Korea, Philippines, and Thailand, including fresh meat, fish, fruit, and vegetables.

If you are ever in the market for a restaurant-size wok, this is the place to go. Actually you'll find almost any size wok and accoutrements here.

Maxim

640 University Boulevard East
Silver Spring MD
301-439-0110

460 Hungerford Drive
Rockville MD
301-279-0110

Monday-Friday 9:30 to 8 / Sunday to 7
Parking available

Maxim has two stores and they are almost overwhelming in variety of products. Both are full-service stores with fresh produce, bakery, fishmonger, meat market, frozen foods, and many, many canned products and utensils.

How about the crow-shaped tooth pick dispenser? Push its head down and out comes a toothpick. Or some dried shark's fin at a hundred dollars or so a pound.

The Rockville store is ultra-modern. Silver Spring operations are more traditional with a restaurant and several "cubicle" stores selling cloth, jewelry, etc., abutting the grocery area.

This is a good place to be introduced to Chinese breads and sweets, which are all baked on the premises. The saucer-size baked yeast buns — plain or filled with coconut, sweetened green bean paste, vanilla custard, butter cream, or roast pork — are wonderful snacks. Consider the moon cakes (pastries filled with sweetened red bean paste, lotus seed and other goodies), the coconut tartlets, giant walnut cookies, and many more.

In the Silver Spring store you'll see barbecued pork loins, ducks, and various parts — maybe even a whole roasted pig sitting forlornly on its haunches.

Mee Wah Lung

608 H Street NW
Washington DC
202-737-0968

Daily 9 to 6 / Tuesday to 2:30
On-street parking / Near Gallery Place subway station

This family enterprise is tucked away in the basement and attended by friendly and helpful people. Here you'll find fresh produce, preserved eggs, lap cheong (sausage), soy and other sauces, woks, tea sets, sesame oil, and several canned, dried, and frozen products.

Among my favorites is the Chinese-style barbecued pork loin (chao siu) made here. You'll see this with similarly cooked chickens and ducks hanging in the display case separating the market from the food staging area in the rear.

The loins are marinated in soy sauce, hoisin sauce, brown bean sauce, rice wine, five-spice powder, garlic, and sugar. Then each loin is hung in an oven and baked until it is a luscious reddish-brown. Take some home and use it in a stir-fry, in cold noodle dishes, or in a sandwich.

On weekends (and for special orders), delightful steamed buns are prepared. Yeasted and filled with a mixture of chopped chao siu, scallions, and hoisin sauce, these buns are perfect as a snack or with a cup of tea.

Oriental Market

891F Rockville Pike
Rockville MD
301-340-8018

Monday-Thursday 10 to 8 / Friday-Saturday 10 to 9
Sunday 10 to 6:30

This supermarket offers a good selection of fresh produce, meat, and fish along with frozen products (lamb, pork, and beef) and many canned and dried products. Don't pass up the frozen Chinese bread products and dumplings.

In China, while you're waiting in line for a movie you're likely to buy a tea egg from a street vendor. Here in the Washington area you'll have to settle for the electric crock pot at the cash register in Oriental Market. They're hard-boiled in tea first. Next the shells are cracked a bit and put back into the tea along with some soy sauce and five-spice powder and allowed to steep and turn dark brown. Now please don't take these into the movies!

For something else novel, try the Asian popsicles. They come in peanut butter, guava, taro root, mango, or red bean paste flavors.

Pacific Market

5900B Leesburg Pike
Falls Church VA
703-671-8727

Monday-Saturday 10 to 9 / Sunday 10 to 8
Parking available

This store started out as one of the Asian Village markets (there's still one in Hyattsville MD). You'll find products from several Asian countries, but the Chinese cuisine is emphasized. Expect to find fresh vegetables and fruits, a extensive selection of fish (maybe some live ones in the large tank), and all kinds of noodles, sauces, vinegars, condiments, and other canned and frozen goods.

More Chinese Markets

Asia Supermarket
6216 Wilson Boulevard
Falls Church VA
703-237-8411

Monday-Saturday 9 to 8
    Sunday 10 to 6:30
Parking available

Fairfax Asian Market
9980 Main Street
Fairfax VA
703-352-2540

Daily 9:30 to 8:30
Parking available

Jade Tree
350 Fortune Terrace
Potomac MD
301-279-9522

Monday-Saturday 10 to 7:30
    Sunday 11 to 7
Parking available

New Asia Market
10028 Darnestown Road
Rockville MD
301-762-0938

Monday-Saturday 10 to 8
    Sunday 10 to 7
Parking available

Taiwan Grocery
4540 Montgomery Avenue
Bethesda MD
301-654-8505

Monday-Saturday 11 to 6
Parking available

French

The French Market

1632 Wisconsin Avenue NW
Washington DC
202-338-4828

Monday-Tuesday & Thursday-Friday 8:30 to 6
Wednesday 8:30 to 1:30
Saturday 7:30 to 6
Parking behind the store

Boucherie-Charcuterie Française declares the window sign. Inside the Brothers Jacob (Robert, Georges, and Jean) display meats cut and trimmed the French Way and scads of other French groceries, including pastries, cheeses, bread, jams, olive oils, and cured meats — all in the nooks and crannies of three side-by-side townhouses.

Robert Jacob started the business in 1957 and quickly began catering to Georgetown notables — offering housemade sausages (campagne fumée, boudin blanc, mergues, and boudin noir) and prepared dishes such as pâté campagne en croûte, cassoulette, chicken cordon bleu, and gallantine en croûte.

You'll also find truffles — two to the can or in shavings — caviar, dried morels, house-made praline paste, crème fraîche, and fresh produce.

You're among friends here, so don't hesitate to ask for advice.

German

Elsie's German Deli

8139 Telegraph Road
Severn MD
410-551-6000

Monday-Friday 9 to 6 / Saturday 9 to 5 / Sunday 11 to 3
Parking available

Elsie's has been around since 1968 and has built up a loyal following among local German-food enthusiasts — bratwurst, liverwurst, and weisswurst are favorites along with rollmops, liverkaese and cheeses imported from Germany and Switzerland. From the Old World Bakery in Baltimore are German rye breads with whole grain, linseed and sunflower seeds, mischbrot (a sour dough and yeast bread) and broetchen (rolls). Bauernbrot (farmers' bread) comes in from New Jersey. Vinegars, sauerkraut, flavored syrups, jams, preserves, fruits in syrup, pickles, mustards, dumpling mixes, and canned fish. German butter, cakes, candies and coffee.

German video cassettes, books, cards, magazines and a few cook books in English. They will put together gift packages and ship for you.

Elsie's German Delicatessen

14531 Jeff Davis Highway
Woodbridge VA
703-494-6919

Monday-Friday 9 to 6 / Saturday 9 to 5
Parking available

If you're not sure you're in the mood for grocery shopping the German music here will change your mind. So put on your lederhosen and go see what Mrs. Cho, originally from Korea, and her German staff have to offer.

You'll find domestic wursts under the Schaller & Weber, Usinger, Gaiser, and Schaffer labels, including blut, zwiebel, jag, gelb, beer, tea, and weiss; hams such as Westphalian, Black Forest, nussschinken, and bauernschinken; smoked shoulder (schinken-speck); landjager; German cheese and butter; and roll-mops.

There are also breads from Canada and Germany, mustards, pickles, Tchibo and Jacobs brand coffee, jams and preserves, canned vegetables, fruits, and fish, and mixes of all sorts. For refreshments, choose from the 15 or so German beers, including the popular Kaiserdom Malz non-alcoholic version. Buy a stein, and a cuckoo clock to go with your beer.

German Deli

1331 H Street NW
Washington DC
202-347-5732

Monday-Friday 7:30 a.m. to 10 p.m. / Saturday 9 a.m. to 10 p.m.
Sunday 11 to 10
On-street parking / Near McPherson Square subway station

In Washington since 1926, German Deli now teams with Mozart Cafe to bring you both take-out and eat-in Austrian and German specialties.

German breads include linseed rye, Klosterbrot, sunflower seed rye. Swedish limpa. Wursts, ham, corned beef, and other meat items. Smoked eel. Canned vegetables and fruits, pickles, sauerkraut, vinegars, and mustards. Prepared foods. Cheeses. Coffee beans. Candies. Cookies. Canned herring of various varieties. Anchovy sprat fillets. Canned and dried soups. Spices and herbs.

During the Christmas season, German Deli has individually wrapped candies for stocking stuffing; yule music on cassette; gift baskets; and marzipan replicas of the Cafe Mozart piano with tasty chocolate centers.

German Gourmet

7185 Lee Highway
Falls Church VA
703-534-1908

Monday-Friday 9 to 7 / Saturday 9 to 6
Parking available

Raimund Pagani has stocked his store just about to the rafters with German-style delicatessen meats, cheeses, pastries (including four kinds of house-made strudels), breads, mixes, canned goods, candies, beer, wine, cookbooks, magazines, and "gifts from the Old Country".

He makes his own bratwurst and gets the rest of his extensive inventory of wursts from Usinger and Schaller and Weber (there are wurz, beer, schinken, zungen, weiss, kalbsrat, sutz — to mention a few). Hams are nuss, bauern, schinkenspeck, Black Forest, Lachs, and Westphalian. Hungarian czerkesz, similar to landjaeger, and a heavily smoked sausage called guilay, also Hungarian, add ethnic variety.

Breads from Canada and Germany include holzofen, linseed, vollkorn, steinofen, and bauern sauer.

Also expect to see pickled herring; canned mushrooms; jams and preserves; sweet and hot Hungarian paprika; German coffee; sugar beet syrup; and several varieties of canned vegetables and fruits.

Wine, Beer, and German Stuff Deli

7 Olney-Sandy Point Road
Ashton MD
301-774-1707

Monday-Saturday 10 to 10 / Sunday 11 to 7
Parking available

Ernie Lichtenstein's deli is in the Ashton Village Center at the intersection of New Hampshire Avenue and Route 108. His "German stuff" consists of a smallish section of grocery items, a deli section of wursts, hams, pickles, sweets, German breads from Canada and Elsie's Bakery in Severn, and a few frozen prepared dishes. Most of the floor space is dedicated to fine wines and hearty beers.

Heidelberg Pastry Shoppe

2150 North Culpeper Street
Arlington VA
703-527-8394

Monday 6:30 to 3 / Tuesday-Friday 6:30 to 6:30
Saturday 8 to 5 / Sunday 8 to 1
Parking available

Primarily a European-style bakery, Heidelberg also stocks German grocery items such as delicatessen meats (wursts, hams, and head cheese); cheese; cucumber pickles; mustard; jams; oils; vinegars; canned mushrooms; nuts; and pickled asparagus. Don't be embarrassed if you decide to stuff your shopping bags with the wonderful breads and sweets here; there are lots of them.

This store is just off the 4800 block of Lee Highway.

Le Grand Appetit

9853 Georgetown Pike
Great Falls VA
703-759-4450

Monday-Friday 9 to 7 / Saturday 9 to 6
Parking available

This gourmet shop and cafe has many German, Italian, and French products. European-style breads are from Bake Aroma bakeries in Chantilly, Virginia. Expect to see wursts, Westphalian ham, Black Forest ham, prosciutto, pastrami, corned beef, chopped liver, sausages, salamis, homemade sauerkraut, cheese, and pastries. Several cookbooks are available.

Wurzburg Haus

7206 Muncaster Mill Road
Rockville MD
301-963-5223

Monday-Saturday 10 to 9
Parking available

Christa and Helmut Kurtz own this Red Mill Shopping Center market and a restaurant of the same name a few doors away. Hearty German breads, cakes, and strudels baked in the restaurant are sold in the market along with imported German breads, cakes, and cookies.

Cheeses consist of limburger, harzekase, and kochkase. There are Hungarian salami, liverwurst, blutwurst, German butter, dried and canned Bavarian cepes and straw mushrooms, several jams, canned fish, mustards, pickles, and sauerkraut.

European Market, a Portuguese store, is across the street.

Greek

Greek markets also sell products for Turkish, Armenian, Iranian, and Arabic cookery. Middle Eastern markets sell many Greek items.

Acropolis Food Market   1206 Underwood Street NW
Washington DC
202-829-1414

Tuesday-Saturday 10 to 7 / Sunday 10 to 3
On-street parking

Anthony Summar, in his stately mid-eighties, likely will be sitting at the cash register regaling customers with tales of Greek food and customs.

The Greek side of this long-time market stocks products from Greece, Italy, Turkey, Egypt, and Lebanon — canned goods, pastas, olives, olive oils, feta and other cheeses, halva, wheat rusks, and lokum. Soujouk, a beef salami, is made in the United States. There is a good selection of Greek wines and cookbooks for the Greek, Middle Eastern, and Ethiopian cuisines. Christopsomo, a yeasted sweet bread, is on hand at Christmas.

About half the products are Ethiopian, including such spices as alicha blends, mitmita eaten with raw beef, awaze for tibs dishes, and berbere for wotts. There are also teff flour, several grains and beans, and locally-made aenjera bread.

Maria's Greek Corner   409 Maple Avenue West
Vienna VA
703-938-3663

Monday-Saturday 10 to 8 / Sunday 11 to 4
Parking available

You'll find Greek, Turkish, Arabic, and Persian products here all peacefully sharing shelf space.

In the refrigerator case you'll see Greek loucanico sausage flavored with a bit of orange rind, Turkish soujouk sausage and pastirma (pastrami), and pork sausage casings. Cookies and sweets under the Apollo brand. Greek, Turkish, and Moroccan olives.

Turkish canned vegetables, jams, juices, olives — Greek cheeses — Greek rye, whole wheat, and other rusks, which are a great favorite in Greece. Greek-style bread in large rings and loaves. Greek vases, "worry" beads, charms, and other gift items round out the selections.

Near Amphora Bakery (Greek), Nizam's Restaurant (Turkish), De Fluri's Bakery (European), and Italian Gourmet Deli — so, enjoy!

Indian / Pakistani

Bismillah Halal Meat Market

1401 University Boulevard West
Langley Park MD
301-434-0051

Monday-Thursday 11 to 8 / Friday 3 to 8
Saturday-Sunday 10 to 8
Parking available

Bismillah has moved from its Holton Lane location to the rear of nearby International Mall. Beef, veal, lamb, goat, and chicken halal-style are available in various sizes and cuts. Good buys too. Indo-Pakistani grocery items are also sold.

Bombay Food & Gifts

11211C Lee Highway
Fairfax VA
703-352-3663

Monday-Saturday 10 to 8 / Sunday 12 to 6
Parking available

Perhaps Surinder Matharoo's nurse training explains the gleam in this new shop. As with most Indian stores, you will find groceries, jewelry, and clothing for sale. But what sets this sparkling store apart from the rest is the delicious cafeteria-style array of homemade hot and cold carryout dishes. Ms. Matharoo makes them all on the premises, including paneer (a fresh whole milk cheese) which she cooks with green peas, potatoes, and Indian spices. This is a fine opportunity to select from several meat and vegetarian dishes. Take some home and then come back and buy the ingredients for your own version. For desserts or tea-time accompaniments, try the Indian sweets shown to their colorful advantage in lighted glass cases, an enticement to sample them all.

A couple of doors away in the same shopping center is Alibi Bakery and its German sweets and breads.

India Foods

1355 Holton Lane
Langley Park MD
301-434-2433

Monday-Saturday 11 to 9 / Sunday 11 to 8
Parking available

Such trademark Indian food products as flat breads, teas, spices, herbs, rice, dals, and various kinds of canned vegetables and fruits are available here. Sweets are from New York. Spicy, fried snack crunchies are great with a beer.

Fresh vegetables usually include ginger root, coriander, okra, eggplant, tubers, and other more exotic specimen. Try some of the frozen prepared dishes if you're not quite ready to try your hand at Indian cooking.

This store is a good source for "Genuine Gathering Spanish Saffron" at rock bottom prices. Ice creams are based on mango, saffron pistachio, jackfruit, coco yam, and green coconut.

Indian Spices and Appliances

3901 Wilson Boulevard
Arlington VA
703-522-0149

Daily 11 to 8:30
Parking available / Near Virginia Square subway station

This store offers a large variety of Indian goods and cook books. Chutneys, locally-made sweets, dals, Indian beer, Tandoori paste, lime pickle, basmati and other rice, rose water, a huge selection of tea from the Assam and Darjeeling areas, spices, and herbs.

From India come entrees in their own boiling pouch. One that I enjoy is the kadi pakora or chickpea dumplings in a spicy yogurt sauce. There are several other dishes to choose from.

Among the fresh produce you may find fresh elephant ear roots, eggplants, long beans, coriander, hot peppers, and bitter melons.

Indian Super Market

8107 Fenton Street
Silver Spring MD
301-589-8417

Daily 11 to 8:30
Parking available

Merchants Adyanand and Pratima Singh sell almost as many Ethiopian products as Indian, undoubtedly due to the number of Ethiopians residing in the area. The full range of spices and grains used so extensively in Ethiopian cookery is represented here. Locally-made aenjera and ambaasha breads are also sold.

Typical Indian fare includes spices and more spices, snack foods, chutneys, pickles, canned vegetables and fruits, dals, grains, fresh produce, sweets, breads, frozen prepared dishes, etc.

My favorite fresh chutneys are those based on mint, coconut, coriander, or dates; there are also garlic and red pepper chutneys, but I've not been brave enough to try those yet. They are wonderful, spicy accompaniments to a wide range of dishes, Indian or otherwise. Look for the special chutney that is poured over bhel mix, a snack food made from toasted rice and chickpea flour tidbits. Quite tasty.

Unique to Indian stores are the dried snacks that puff up after a few seconds in hot oil. These thin circles, pinwheels, squares, and sticks and are known by several names such as rice sev, rice papad, far far, urad papad, and potato rackets. Consisting of rice, dal, and potato flours and flavored with assertive Indian spices, they make outstanding hors d'oeuvres.

In the frozen food case you'll see several ready-made dishes such as aloo matar (potato and sweet pea stew), aloo began (potatoes and eggplants), rogan josh (lamb curry), dal masala curry, chicken curry, and palak paneer (cheese and spinach).

For bread, expect to find whole wheat chapati, mint parotha, masala parotha, roti, and onion kulcha.

In late 1991, the Singhs redesigned their store and made half of it into a jewelry store.

Indo-Pak Spices

424 Elden Street
Herndon VA
703-425-9415

Monday-Saturday 10 to 8:30 / Sunday 11 to 6:30
Parking available

Groceries and fabrics are the centerpieces at this new store. You will find good selections of bagged snacks based on seasoned and fried chickpeas, dals, nuts, and "noodles"; mixes, including those for preparing jilebi, dhokla, vadai, idli, pakora, and dosai; all sorts of pickles and chutneys; fresh vegetables; frozen dinners; sweets; and various types of bread, highlighted by the spicy papad, which, when fried, puffs up into a delicious party snack. Look for dried ginger root and grind your own ginger powder.

International Super Market & Halal Meat

1545 Rockville Pike
Rockville MD
301-816-9811

Monday-Saturday 11 to 8:30 / Sunday 11 to 7
Parking available

This 1991 arrival features Indian and Pakistani staples, fresh fruits and vegetables, and "100% Muslim Way Halal" meat, including whole lambs and goats. It's in Congressional Plaza North.

Muskan

956 Thayer Avenue
Silver Spring MD
301-588-0331

Monday-Saturday 11 to 8 / Sunday 11 to 6
Metered parking nearby

Perfectly aligned in rows like tin soldiers on toy store shelves stand containers of Indian pickles, chutneys, pastes, and curry sauces — biryani, vindaloo, moghlai, tikka, and Madras are a few of the styles. Nearby are rice, dals, nuts, ghee, almond and cashew butters, canned vegetables and fruits, those famous crunchy, fried Indian snacks, and a couple of cookbooks.

With some 25 different frozen vegetarian dishes available you should be able to eat Indian style for quite a while. As an accompaniment try the exotic prawn pickles or the fresh coconut, mint, or coriander chutneys. For breads there are pita, nan, chapati, and roti. And dessert could be chum-chum, a delicious little sandwich made entirely of milk and cream lightly bathed with a sugar syrup and topped with crushed pistachios.

Muskan ("smile" in Hindi) is up the street from Thai Market and across from Negril Bakery (Jamaican).

More Indian/Pakistani Markets

Apna Bazaar
10119C Washington Blvd.
Laurel MD
301-498-1233

Monday-Friday 11 to 7:30
Saturday-Sunday 11 to 8
Parking available

Arlington Grocery & Halal Meat
3425 Wilson Boulevard
Arlington VA
703-527-9720

Daily 9:30 to 9
Friday 2 to 9
Parking available

Asian Food Mart
6550J Little River Turnpike
Alexandria VA
703-256-6565

Daily 9 to 9
Parking available

Asian Gift & Spices
8172 Richmond Highway
Alexandria VA
703-360-5272

Tuesday-Saturday 11 to 8
Sunday-Monday 12 to 6
Parking available

Bharat
4231C Markham Street
Annandale VA
703-256-9267

Monday 3:30 to 7:30
Tuesday-Saturday 11 to
7:30 / Sunday Noon to 6
Parking available

Bombay Store
7033 Spring Garden Drive
Springfield VA
703-569-6777

Monday-Saturday 11 to 8
Parking available

Bombay Super Bazaar

1079 Rockville Pike
Rockville MD
301-424-8081

Monday-Saturday 11 to 7
Sunday 12 to 6
Parking available

Dana Bazar

1701K Rockville Pike
Rockville MD
301-231-7546

Monday-Saturday 11 to 8
Sunday 11 to 7
Parking available

Delhi Bazar

4010 Maury Place
Alexandria VA
703-360-5844

Monday-Saturday 11 to 8
Sunday 12:30 to 6:30
Parking available

Crescent Grocery & Halal

2105 North Pollard Street
Arlington VA
703-243-0444

Saturday-Thursday 11 to 8
Friday 2:30 to 8
Parking available

Dana Bazar

8845 Greenbelt Road
Greenbelt MD
301-552-4400

Tuesday-Sunday 11 to 8:30
Parking available

Exotic India

593 Hungerford Drive
Rockville MD
301-340-9345

Sunday-Friday 11 to 8
Saturday 9 to 9
Parking available

Express Food & Appliances
7453 Annapolis Road
Landover Hills MD
301-459-4059

Tuesday-Saturday 10 to 8
Sunday 12 to 6
Parking available

I. G. Int'l Foods
2630 Columbia Pike
Arlington VA
703-920-3099

Monday-Saturday 11 to 8
Sunday 11 to 4:30
On-street parking

India Bazaar
10557 Greenbelt Road
Lanham MD
301-464-0505

Daily 11 to 8
Parking available

India Emporium
6848 New Hampshire Ave.
Takoma Park MD
301-270-3322

Wednesday-Monday 10 to 8
Parking available

Halal Meat & Spices
4231Q Markham Street
Annandale VA
703-941-8395

Monday-Saturday 10 to 9
Sunday 10 to 8
Parking available

India Bazaar
9045 Gaither Road
Gaithersburg MD
301-840-9799

Daily 11 to 8
Parking available

India Connection
6353 Rolling Road
Springfield VA
703-644-5591

Monday-Saturday 11 to 8
Sunday 12 to 6
Parking available

Indian/Persian Mkt
156B Enterprise Street
Sterling VA
703-450-5531

Daily 11 to 9
Parking available

Indian Super Store
1327D Rockville Pike
Rockville MD
301-424-4877

Monday-Saturday 11 to 8
Sunday 12 to 7
Parking available

International Bazaar
8004B Alban Road
Springfield VA
703-455-3033

Daily 11:30 to 8
Parking available

International Groceries
2109 Mt. Vernon Avenue
Alexandria VA
703-549-7788

Monday-Saturday 11 to 9
Sunday 12 to 6
On-street parking

Indus Food
15535 New Hampshire Ave.
Silver Spring MD
301-989-9448

Tuesday-Saturday 11 to 9
Sunday 11 to 7
Parking available

International Bazar
5129 Lee Highway
Arlington VA
703-533-8736

Monday-Saturday 11 to 8
Sunday 11 to 6
Parking available

International Grocery & Deli
9643 Lee Highway
Fairfax VA
703-591-1599

Tuesday-Saturday 10 to 8
Sunday-Monday 11 to 6
Parking available

International House

765H Rockville Pike
Rockville MD
301-279-2121

Monday-Thursday 11:30 to 8
    Friday 11:30 to 9
    Saturday 11 to 8
    Sunday 12 to 8
Parking available

International Store

3709 Columbia Pike
Arlington VA
703-979-6262

Daily 4 p.m. to 8
Parking available behind
    the store

New York Dana Bazar

1810 University Blvd East
Hyattsville MD
301-439-5772

Tuesday-Sunday 11:30 to 8
Parking available

International Market

14400 Layhill Road
Silver Spring MD
301-598-4115

Daily 6 a.m. to 11 p.m.
Parking available

Khyber Halal Market

5216 Wilson Boulevard
Arlington VA
703-525-8323

Daily 10 a.m. to 10:30 p.m.
Parking available

Patel Brothers

2080 University Blvd East
Langley Park MD
301-422-1555

Tuesday-Sunday 10:30 to 8
Parking available

Patel Brothers
808 Hungerford Drive
Rockville MD
301-340-8656

Daily 10:30 to 8
Parking available

Priya
438 South Washington Street
Falls Church VA
703-534-2558

Tuesday-Saturday 11:30 to 8
Sunday 11:30 to 6
Parking available

Sadana Int'l
6857 New Hampshire Ave.
Langley Park MD
301-270-2443

Monday, Wednesday-Friday
11 to 9 / Saturday 10 to 9
Sunday 10 to 8
Parking available

Pooja Spices
298 Sunset Park Drive
Herndon VA
703-471-4378

Monday-Saturday 11 to 8:30
Sunday 11 to 6:30
Parking available

Sabah Halal Meat
1366 Holton Lane
Langley Park MD
301-434-8282

Daily 10 to 9
Parking available

Shama Spices
13830 Lee Highway
Centreville VA
703-803-6514

Monday-Wednesday 12 to 8
Thursday-Saturday 11 to
8 / Sunday 12 to 6
Parking available

Shanta Store

11137 Georgia Avenue
Wheaton MD
301-942-7883

Monday-Friday 4:30 p.m. to
    8:30 / Saturday-Sunday
    12 to 8

Super Halal
Meat Market

7046 Spring Garden Drive
Springfield VA
703-451-5556

Monday-Saturday 10 to 9
    Sunday 11 to 8
Public metered parking
    nearby

Tu-Tu Market

3811S S. Geo. Mason Drive
Falls Church VA
703-998-5322

Monday-Saturday 10 to 8
    Sunday 10 to 6
Parking available

Sharieff Halal
Meat Market

5135 Lee Highway
Arlington VA
703-536-4322

Monday-Thursday 11 to 8
    Friday 3 to 9 / Saturday
    10 to 9 / Sunday 10 to 6
Parking available

Surya Sweets
and Spices

4941 Harford Avenue
Beltsville MD
301-937-4433

Monday 4 to 8
    Tuesday-Sunday 11 to 8
Parking available

Usman Halal Meat
& Asian Groceries

(Food Factory)
4221 North Fairfax Drive
Arlington VA
703-527-7144

Daily 11 to 11
Parking available

Italian

Italia

8662 Colesville Road
Silver Spring MD
301-588-6999

Monday-Friday 9 to 7 / Saturday 9 to 6
On-street parking / Near Silver Spring subway station

Maria Fortini cooks her pastas and sauces the old-fashioned way — a pinch of this, a little of that. A spoon and delicately attuned taste buds tell her when things taste just right. Besides the numerous pastas, this mom-and-pop delicatessen and salumeria has its own housemade sweet and hot Italian sausage links, sfogliatelle, and cannoli. At Easter, Ms. Fortini makes pastiera. Panetonne is imported for Christmas.

On the shelves are typical Italian canned goods, dry pasta, olive oils, vinegars, and so forth. In the meat case is a good selection of Italian processed meats, including salami and prosciutto; bulk olives; and cheese (mozzarella is made daily). For dessert, try the spumoni or tartuffo ice cream balls.

Italian Gourmet Deli

505 Maple Avenue West
Vienna VA
703-938-4141

Monday-Friday 10 to 7 / Saturday 9 to 7 / Sunday 10 to 5
Parking available

They should bottle the inviting aroma that permeates this sparkling, compact shop. It certainly puts you in the mood to fill several bags full of the prepared pasta dishes, cheeses, prosciutto and other cured meats, canned goods, cookies, ice cream, and all sorts of pastas.

Mozzarella cheese is made on the premises, as are sausages, cannoli, salads, and specialty breads (pepperoni, prosciutto and spinach, and others).

The next time you go to a Wolf Trap concert, stop by here and pick up a picnic. Wine, glasses, utensils, and all the accoutrements can be included. They do gift baskets, too.

Litteri's

57 Morse Street NE
Washington DC
202-544-0184

Monday-Wednesday 8 to 4 / Thursday-Friday 8 to 5
Saturday 8 to 3
Parking available

Litteri's is the grand old man of Washington's Italian stores. It's been around since 1926 and has just about everything you need in Italian products. The meat and cheese counter is tended by grandfatherly types in white aprons — with perhaps a smudge here and there to add to the authenticity. Tasting is encouraged; if you don't know exactly which cheese to select discuss the issue with the counterman. After a few samples you'll be able to choose intelligently. They make their own sausage, which sell for less than supermarket prices.

Expect to see a large selection of canned goods and deli meats; bulk olives; olive oils and vinegars; bread from Catania bakery; fresh, frozen, and dry pasta; frozen sauces and pasta dishes — try the agniolotti stuffed with pesto; cheese; candies; frozen desserts such as tiramisu; and wine. Cook books and serving dishes, too.

This store is located in the northeast wholesale market area near Florida Avenue and Fifth Street NE.

Little Italy Deli

13850E Braddock Road
Centreville VA
703-830-3354

Monday-Thursday 10 to 9 / Friday-Saturday 10 to 10
Sunday 11 to 8
Parking available

In this upscale deli/market you can buy all the components of a quick Italian spaghetti dinner — tomato sauce, made on the premises with fresh basil; several types of pasta under the labels of De Cecco, Pastene, Conte Luna, and Don Peppe; imported parmigiano reggiano; locally-made Italian bread; cannoli; and espresso coffee by Lavazza.

You'll also see the typical canned foods (fish, tomatoes, lupini, peppers); Italian meats such as sweet or spicy sausages, mortadello, sopressata, pancetta, Genoa salami, cappacolla, and imported prosciutto; cheeses, including imported provolone and locatelli, and fresh mozzarella. Olive oil is by Berio, Colavita, and Madre Sicilia.

Owner Bob Orsa says he occasionally has luganega, a mild sausage with coarsely ground meat in a long, narrow casing (good sauteed with mushrooms and a little wine). For the holidays he brings in baccalá (salted cod).

Mamma Lucia's

2409 University Boulevard West
Wheaton MD
301-949-2112

Monday-Saturday 8 to 8 / Sunday 8:30 to 4
Parking available

Old-fashioned and authentic, Mamma Lucia keeps her customers well-supplied with Italian canned goods, dried and frozen pasta, and frozen pizza shells. Prepared dishes, bread, cannoli, and sausages are made on the premises.

This downtown Wheaton store has a good supply of cured meats, pickles, olives, Italian-style salads, cookies, and all sorts of dishes, coffee makers, utensils, and gift items.

Five or so tables offer you the opportunity to sit and enjoy some of the good Italian sandwiches and sweets put together in her deli section.

Mangialardo's

1317 Pennsylvania Ave SE
Washington DC
202-543-6212

Monday-Friday 9 to 3
On-street parking
One block from Potomac Avenue subway station

This market has been around since the early 1950's and is now under second-generation management. It's a small place, but it has a reasonable selection of products, including sausage made on the premises, cold cuts, dried pasta products, olive oils, spices, and canned goods. Bread is from Catania Bakery.

Marcella
La Bersagliera

8540 Connecticut Avenue
Chevy Chase MD
301-951-1818

Monday-Saturday 9 to 9
Parking at the rear of the store

This attractive delicatessen and cafe has both an upscale and old-country air, with the lilt of Italian accents adding to its charm. There is a good selection of cheeses (fontina, gorgonzola, gruviera, bertolli, ricotta, Pecorina, smoked mozzarella, feta) and cold cuts (salami, prosciutto, mortadella, pancetta, coteghini). Other items consist of Moroccan, Sicilian, Gaeta, Calamatta olives; olive oil; Italian coffee; arborio rice; vinegars; and imported baby clams. Desserts include sfogliatelle, cannoli, spumoni, and chocolate-covered tartuffo.

Made in-house are sausage; mozzarella; tomato, meat, Amatriciana, rabbit, pesto, and walnut pasta sauces; and prepared pasta dishes (tortellini, ravioli, gnocchi, and several others).

Marchones

11224 Triangle Lane
Wheaton MD
301-949-4150

Monday-Saturday 9 to 7 / Sunday 10 to 2
Parking available in metered public lot across the lane.

In business since the 1950's, Marchones has a variety of olive oils, cheeses, herbs and spices, bread, canned goods, frozen and dried pasta, olives, sausages made on the premises, and the typical Italian cured meat products and prepared dishes. Rounding out the selections are wines, cannoli, spumoni, cookies, candies, and Italian ices.

Expect to find here whatever ingredients you need for your Italian meal, as well as several types of serving dishes.

The Deli

480 Elden Street
Herndon VA
703-435-9085

Monday-Saturday 10 to 9
Parking available

The trademarks of Italian delis — meat, cheese, and pasta — are here is respectable quantities and consist of imported and domestic prosciutto, dry cappacollo, Genoa Di Lusso, soppressata, pancetta, pepperoni, mortadella, smoked and fresh sausage, pastrami, prosciuttini, parmigiano reggiano, auricchio, fresh mozzarella, locatelli, provolone, fontinella, gorgonzola, and bel paese.

Pasta comes in a multiplicity of shapes, including ditalini, ziti, mostaccioli, tortellini, fusilli, cavatelli, spiretti, and fettucine.

Cannoli is made on the premises; bread; candies (try the baci, chopped hazelnuts and chocolate paste topped with a whole hazelnut and coated with bitter chocolate); desserts (rich and creamy tiramisu, for example); wines; and the other standard Italian grocery items.

Three Brothers
Italian Market

4521 Kenilworth Avenue
Bladensburg MD
301-864-1570

Monday-Saturday 10 to 9 / Sunday 12 to 5
Parking available

Need olive oil or parmesan? Look in the market. Cannoli? Look in the bakery. Not in the mood for cooking? Try the dining room or pizzeria — or have them cater an affair. If this is tiring you, have a drink in the lounge. Horizontal integration is the theme at Three Brothers.

In the warehouse-style market you'll see the standard olive oils, canned goods, dry pasta, condiments, and other Italian products. What sets this place apart is the large collection of dishes and utensils needed to prepare and serve Italian food — pizza pans of all sizes, ravioli makers, cannoli tubes, parmesan cheese graters, fry pans, sauce pots, pasta platters, coffee makers, and so forth.

There are, of course, several types of cold cuts, cheeses, salads, and frozen prepared dishes.

During the Christmas season, they will put together gift baskets.

More Italian Markets

Angelo's Italian Deli
15527 New Hampshire Ave.
Silver Spring MD
301-622-4430

Monday-Thursday & Satur-
   day 9 to 7 / Friday 9 to 8
Parking available

Bozelli Brothers
6691 Backlick Road
Springfield VA
703-451-6411

9306 Richmond Highway
Lorton VA
703-339-5242

Monday-Thursday 9 to 6
   Friday 9 to 7 / Saturday 9
   to 5
Parking available

Gallo's Italian Grocery
6342 Marlboro Pike
Forestville MD
301-568-5444

Monday-Saturday 9 to 5
    Sunday 10 to 3
Parking available

Marinelli's
2506 University Blvd. East
Hyattsville MD
301-422-8422

Monday-Saturday 9 to 8
Parking available

Italian Store
Seven Corners Center
6201 Arlington Boulevard
Falls Church VA
703-241-9193

Monday-Saturday 9:30 to 9
    Sunday 12 to 5
Parking available

3123 Lee Highway
Arlington VA
703-528-6266

Monday-Friday 10 to 7:30
    Saturday 10 to 7 / Sunday
    12 to 6
Parking available

Prego
210 Seventh Street SE
Washington DC
202-547-8686

Monday-Thursday 10 to 6
    Friday 10 to 7 / Saturday
    9 to 6
On-street parking / Near
    Eastern Market subway
    station

3821 S. Geo. Mason Drive
Falls Church VA
703-578-0040

Monday-Thursday 9 to 7
    Friday 9 to 8 / Saturday 9
    to 7
Parking available

Prego Segondo
1617 17th Street NW
Washington DC
202-745-7007

Monday-Saturday 10 to 8
On-street parking

The Deli
4074 Jermantown Road
Fairfax VA
703-591-8511

Monday-Thursday 10 to 7
Friday 10 to 9
Saturday 10 to 7
Parking available

Santucci's
10107 Colesville Road
Silver Spring MD
301-593-8338

Monday-Saturday 9 to 8
Sunday 10 to 3
Parking available

Vace
7010 Wisconsin Avenue
Bethesda MD
301-654-6367

Monday-Saturday 11:30 to 6
Parking available

7601 Air Park Road
Gaithersburg MD
301-926-2414

Monday-Saturday 11:30 to 6
Parking available

3504 Connecticut Ave NW
Washington DC
202-363-1999

Monday-Wednesday 9 to 8
Thursday-Saturday 9 to 9
On-street parking / Near
Cleveland Park subway
station

Viareggio's

3740 12th Street NE
Washington DC
202-526-5103

Tuesday-Saturday 8:30 to 6
   Sunday 9 to 3
On-street parking

Vignola Pasta Gourmet

113A N. Washington Street
Rockville MD
301-340-2350

Monday-Friday 9 to 7
   Saturday 9 to 6
Parking available

Japanese

Daruma

1749 Rockville Pike
Rockville MD
301-881-6966

Wednesday-Monday 10 to 7
Parking available

Formerly Fortune Cookie, Daruma is a small store featuring Japanese canned goods, fresh fish for sushi, several frozen products, a small selection of fresh produce, and a lending library. Near Magruder's at Congressional Plaza.

Mikado

4709 Wisconsin Avenuc NW
Washington DC
202-362-7700

Tuesday-Saturday 9:30 to 6:30 / Sunday 10 to 6
On-street parking / Near Tenley Circle subway station

This 25-year-old store and its associated Mikado restaurant have well-established reputations among Washington area residents. In the market you will find tuna, flounder, yellow tail, sea urchins, salmon, jumbo clam, and cuttlefish for sushi and sashimi. If you wish to buy assembled sushi, owner, Mr. Tokuji Iwai, suggests you order ahead since the restaurant puts this together for the store. There's split semi-dried horse mackerel which the Japanese broil before eating. They also sell thinly sliced beef and pork for suki-yaki.

A full line of fresh produce often includes daikon radish sprouts, beefsteak leaves, enoki and shiitake mushrooms, cucumbers, taro root, eggplants, water cress, Asian cabbages and radishes, burdock, and Japanese yams. An Asian cucumber pickle is soaked in a mixture of rice powder, beans, salt, chili peppers, and kelp; quite tasty when eaten as a condiment. Be sure to wash the marinade off before eating the pickle. You can buy both the cucumbers and the soaking medium here, but the instructions for using are in Japanese.

New Wave Seafood   3821 South George Mason Drive
Falls Church VA
703-379-9444

Monday-Saturday 10:30 to 8 / Sunday 1 to 7
Parking available

This upscale fish market and sushi bar offers several kinds of fresh fish and frozen products and a small selection of Japanese grocery items.

Fresh salmon, tuna, catfish, scallops, flounder, swordfish, monkfish, shad roe, sea urchin roe, red snapper, mussels, oysters, clams, and grouper — in season. Live lobsters and rainbow trout. Frozen eel and squid from Japan. Dried sardines and shaved bonito. Small selection of rice and sauces. Dried seaweed. Cookbooks for sushi and other Japanese dishes.

Sakura Books & Foods

15809 South Frederick Road
Rockville MD
301-948-5112

Tuesday-Saturday 10 to 7 / Sunday 10 to 6
Parking available

Enter through the book section and take a look at the cook books and a few other books in English. In the store's rear spend a while looking over the canned, frozen, and dried food products and several gift and utensil items. Notice the design of the containers — especially the candy and the salad dressing bottles. The "bread crumb," wonderful crunchy crumbs, are much larger than the Western versions and are excellent for tempura. Try the Blue Berry, Green Gum (mint), and coffee-flavored chewing gums.

Korean

Fairfax Oriental Store

8630A Lee Highway
Fairfax VA
703-876-4615

Tuesday-Friday 10 to 9:30 / Saturday 9:30 to 9:30
Sunday 9:30 to 8
Parking available

Korean products predominate at this pleasant store, however there are sizeable selections of Chinese and Japanese foodstuffs. Some interesting selections are small rice-flour ovals (used as a soup filler); frozen kimchee dumplings that take about five minutes to steam or fry (instructions on the package); and the tall slender cans of carbonated barley soda with a delicious taste of roasted barley. The Koreans also make a nice tea from the roasted barley.

Korean Korner

12207 Viers Mill Road
Wheaton MD
301-933-2000

Daily 9 a.m. to 10 p.m.
Parking available

This is a large store with a good selection of meats, side dishes, and packaged ingredients for Korean meat- and fish-based dishes put together in the store. You'll find beef for such Korean dishes as short ribs and bulgogi. It's so attractively displayed that you may even find yourself going here for your American beef-based cooking. There are also pork and chicken.

Korean Korner has a large collection of the famous Korean side dishes, which you serve yourself salad-bar-style. These side dishes resemble Western condiments, although the ingredients are somewhat exotic — garlic bulbs, raw crabs, baby octopi, fish intestines, seaweed, each marinated in a dressing of soy sauce, chili pepper, garlic, etc. They're not all so unusual, though, and you may find some of them interesting eaten with a simple bowl of rice to offset their assertive flavors.

The custom-packaged vegetables and meat or fish are real time-savers for a hot-pot or Korean stew. You merely find a recipe for the dish (the name is shown on the package) and you're all set without having to buy more than you need of each individual product. Kop chang jun gol and kop chang ku-i are both tripe-based packages; yuk gae jang is beef based and there is a fish-based selection containing fish, a clam, cabbage, sprouts, onions, and something with the intriguing name of dropwort.

This is a good place to buy kim bap, a seaweed-covered cylinder of rice surrounding a center of colorful vegetables, meat, or fish. When the cylinder is cut into one-inch slices you have a beautiful dark green outside, a white rice layer, and then the color of whatever components are placed in the center.

Lotte Oriental Supermarket

11790 Parklawn Drive
Rockville MD
301-881-3355

3250 Old Lee Highway
Fairfax VA
703-352-1600

Daily 10 to 9
Parking available

It took about two years for Rockville's sister store to open in Fairfax, but the wait was worth it, and I think the new store surpasses its sibling. Both stores are large, immaculate, and bright. At every visit I head for the produce section where outstanding fresh Asian vegetables and fruits await.

If you can get through the vegetables with enough room left in your shopping cart, be sure you stop at the side-dish bar and load up plastic containers with whatever kimchee or other dish strikes your fancy. At one time in Rockville you could sample the dishes with toothpicks, but apparently the food inspectors didn't care too much for that approach and the toothpicks had to be put away.

Then on to the seafood section and beyond to the bustling counters where cuts of meat are being fashioned and to-go dishes being made ready. On the weekends there will be someone baking little sweets in the Rockville store. During one of my visits, Japanese obang cakes were being made in hot cast-iron molds. The mold with small fish shapes engraved into it opens up into two sides. Into both sides go a layer of pancake batter. While these are firming up, some lightly sweetened bean paste and a few pine nuts are put on top of one side. The mold is closed and in a few minutes out comes a small browned fish-shaped cake. If you're not used to Japanese sweets you may find them a bit understated, but they could be a conversation piece at your next tea party.

Lucky World Supermarket

3109 Graham Road (at route 50)
Falls Church VA
703-641-8585

14222 Cherry Lane Court
Laurel MD
410-604-8585

Daily 9:30 to 9:30 / Sunday to 8:30
Parking available

Froot Loops and bean paste. Peanut butter and kimchee. The Falls Church Lucky World is about 20,000 square feet of Korean and American groceries along with lesser quantities of Japanese, Vietnamese, Chinese, and Latin American products. It's across the street from Loehman's Plaza on route 50 in a former Safeway store. You can spend hours here with your Korean cookbook looking up products and how to cook them. Then you use one of the five check-out lanes to settle up.

If you're searching for a Korean ingredient and can't find it here, you're not likely to find it anywhere in the metropolitan area — three 60-foot shelves of bean pastes; similar stocks of noodles, dried fish, rice, dumplings, and dried hot pepper; gallons and gallons of kimchee, that delicious fermented condiment made from cabbage or other vegetables; frozen seafood from esoteric sea squirt to the more familiar oyster; fresh meat and fish; and a Korean side-dish bar where you can select various spicy seafood and vegetable dishes.

The Laurel store is not as large, but makes up for it by having more personal service. Ask for Mrs. Chang Inhwa if you need help. This market is just off Route 1 and across the street from Pace Warehouse.

More Korean Markets

Asia House
1576 Annapolis Road
Odenton MD
301-674-5500

Tuesday-Sunday 9 to 9
Parking available

Arlington Korea House
2700 North Pershing Drive
Arlington VA
703-522-3600

Monday and Wednesday-
    Saturday 9:30 to 9:30
    Sunday 10 to 10
On-street parking

Asian Food Market
615 South Frederick Avenue
Gaithersburg MD
301-948-1344

Tuesday-Saturday 9:30 to 9
    Sunday 9:30 to 7
Parking available

Asian Gourmet Foods
12337B Georgia Avenue
Silver Spring MD
301-949-1177

Monday-Saturday 10 to 10
    Sunday 10 to 8
Parking available

Brown's Oriental Grocery
3537 Ft. Meade Road
Laurel MD
410-792-8990

Tuesday-Saturday 10 to 9
    Sunday 11 to 8
Parking available

Han Yang Oriental Food
4215 Annandale Center Dr.
Annandale VA
703-354-7748

Monday 9:30 to 9:30
    Wednesday-Saturday 9:30
    to 9:30 / Sunday 11 to 8
Parking available

Korea House
4231N Markham Street
Annandale VA
703-354-1515

Daily 9:30 to 9:30
    Tuesday and Sunday to 8
Parking available

New Seoul
1555 Rockville Pike
Rockville MD
301-770-7870

Monday 11 to 8 / Tuesday-
    Saturday 10 to 9 / Sunday
    10 to 8
Parking available

Oriental House
7816 Richmond Highway
Alexandria VA
703-360-0533

Monday-Saturday 9:30
    to 9:30
    Sunday 9:30 to 9
Parking available

Manna Market
7123 Columbia Pike
Annandale VA
703-642-8549

Daily 9:30 to 9:30
Parking available

Oriental Food Town
8174 Richmond Highway
Alexandria VA
703-360-5505

Monday-Saturday 9 to 9
    Sunday 9 to 8
Parking available

Oriental Market
6343A Rolling Road
Springfield VA
703-451-5929

Monday and Wednesday-
    Saturday 10 to 9
    Sunday 10:30 to 7:30
Parking available

Oriental Seoul Market
13662 Jeff Davis Highway
Woodbridge VA
703-491-6967

Monday-Saturday 10 to 9
    Sunday 11 to 6
Parking available

Shin Ja Oriental Grocery
1690E Annapolis Road
Odenton MD
410-674-4556

Daily 9 to 9
Parking available

Yang Ja Market
7918 Georgia Avenue
Silver Spring MD
301-587-0006

Monday-Saturday 10 to 10
    Sunday 10 to 8
Parking available behind the
    store / enter from alley
    off Eastern Avenue.

Sam-Mi
6674 Arlington Boulevard
Falls Church VA
703-532-2066

Monday & Wednesday-
    Sunday 10 to 10:30
Parking available

Y. & G. Oriental Mart
4634 Suitland Road
Suitland MD
301-568-1113

Tuesday-Saturday 9:30
    to 7:30 / Sunday 10 to 7
Parking available

Laotian

Soukanh Oriental Market

7507 Presidential Lane
Manassas VA
703-368-3454

Monday-Friday 9 to 8 / Saturday 10 to 7:30
Sunday 10 to 6:30
Parking available

Soukanh Sayavongsa came to America from Laos in 1982 and opened his market in 1988. It's in Ambassador Square just off Route 28 where the latter goes under Route 66. Here is a good place to try bananas preserved with honey. Soukanh has dried persimmons from Malaysia, fresh pomelos in season, and all sorts of frozen and canned products.

The frozen Laotian pork sausage, made in the United States with lemon grass, garlic, and black pepper, is a tasty dish when sauteed over low heat for 20 minutes or so. I understand this is eaten uncooked in Laos.

More exotic are the dried poo leaves and betel bark. It is said that the elderly in Laos chew this and then use the dried bai ya to clean their teeth. Picturesque are the silver dollar-size fish cakes that have been fried, skewered, and dried. This is traveling food; so, the next time you need sustenance on that ski trip, drop by and pick up a pack.

For something a bit more ethnic than the electric rice cookers you see everywhere, you might try the straw baskets and pot-bellied aluminum pots for sale here. The basket sits atop the pot and holds rice for steaming.

Latin American

These markets sell food products used in countries from Mexico to the tip of South America and in the Spanish-speaking Caribbean. The Latin American stores also sell West Indian and West African food products. Likewise, most West Indian and West African stores will sell Latin American products.

Americana Grocery

1500 University Boulevard East
Hyattsville MD
301-434-8922

6128 Columbia Pike
Falls Church VA
703-671-9625

8541 Piney Branch Road
Silver Spring MD
301-495-0864

1813 Columbia Road NW
Washington DC
202-265-7455

4900 Annapolis Road
Bladensburg MD
301-864-4870

Bladensburg:　Monday-Saturday 8:30 to 7:30 / Sunday 8:30 to 4
Falls Church:　Monday, Tuesday & Saturday 9 to 7
　　　　　　　Wednesday-Friday 9 to 7:30 / Sunday 9 to 3
Hyattsville:　Monday-Thursday 8:30 to 7:30
　　　　　　　Friday 8:30 to 8:30 / Sunday 8 to 3:30
Silver Spring:　Monday-Saturday 9 to 8 / Sunday 8:30 to 4
Washington:　Monday-Saturday 8:30 to 7 / Sunday 8:30 to 5

Parking available at all stores

Americana has added a fifth store (Bladensburg) since the first edition of this guide. This chain store operation specializes in large stores — the Washington operation is not as large as the others — with a full selection of grocery products for Latin American cooking. All the stores have fresh meat and produce, frozen products, prepared dishes, breads, sweets, herbs, and spices.

Casa Lebrato

1733 Columbia Road NW
Washington DC
202-234-0099

Monday-Saturday 8 to 7:30 / Sunday 8:30 to 6
On-street parking

Owners Ruben Capote and Jose Marin, originally from Cuba, and staff will be happy to help you select ingredients for your Latin American cooking. The store specializes in Salvadoran products, but it has many things from the other Latin American countries, the West Indies, and West Africa. Ruben suggests you try their tender beef that's specially cut for great fajitas.

You'll also find green plantains for frying up a side dish of tostones; they have them frozen ready-made also. I like them as chips, too, and my favorite is a spicy version imported from El Salvador.

Casa Peña

1636 17th Street NW
Washington DC
202-462-2222

Daily 8 a.m. to midnight
On-street parking / Four blocks from Q Street subway station

After many years in cramped and dim quarters, Casa Peña expanded into space next door in the fall of 1991; the old part of the store is the meat department. It's now a modern supermarket, although not as large as the SUPERmarkets. There are fresh produce, fresh meat, frozen goods, and many other products.

El Chaparral
Meat Market

1737 Wilson Boulevard
Arlington VA
703-527-3388

2719 Wilson Boulevard
Arlington VA
703-276-8337

Monday-Saturday 10 to 7 / Sunday 10 to 2
Parking available

Another case of success breeding expansion. El Chapparal is now in two locations, and separated by only ten blocks. As might be surmised by the name, meat is a central feature here. However, there are also good selections of fresh produce; canned products; dried beans, grains, and pastas.

La Cuzcatleca
Grocery Store

14412 Jeff Davis Highway
Woodbridge VA
703-490-4907

Monday-Friday 10 to 9 / Saturday 9 to 9 / Sunday 9 to 8
Parking available

This bright and tidy store, with a travel agency tucked away in a corner, opened in 1990. It has products from most of the Latin American countries, including mazamorra morada, sweet potato flour, and dried clams from Peru, Bolivian dried potatoes, and Mexican chocolate. There's also a sizeable selection of Andean herbs and spices as well as fresh meat, chorizos, and fresh produce.

La Quesaria

2412 18th Street NW
Washington DC
202-232-1100

Daily 10 to 8
On-street parking

Washington now has a cheese shop specializing in Salvadoran-style cheese and other dairy products. Owner Hector Roos, from Peru, makes all the products at his plant in Delaware.

Unless you've familiar with Salvadoran cheeses you'll need an introduction by the staff. Expect to hear a lot of "similar to's" — requeson similar to ricotta, a deep yellow cheese similar to cheddar, etc. Other products include fresh butter; mozzarella; cow's milk feta; fresh American-, Salvadoran-, and Mexican-style cream; fresh chorizos; and sweet corn tamales wrapped in corn husks. There are also a few canned goods.

Las Americas

8651 16th Street
Silver Spring MD
301-588-0882

785 Rockville Pike
Rockville MD
301-424-9550

Silver Spring:	Monday-Friday 11 to 9 / Saturday 8 to 8
			Sunday 8 to 4 / Parking available
Rockville:		Monday 11 to 8 / Tuesday-Saturday 10 to 8
			Sunday 10 to 4 / Parking available

Products include Mexican corn husks for tamales; frozen banana leaves from the Philippines; frozen prepared dishes; frozen yuca, cassava, crema de maiz, and gandules; cheese, fresh meat and chorizos; canned goods; fresh produce; several types of yerba mate from Argentina; and dried Spanish figs.

Surtidora Mexicana

13732 Jeff Davis Highway
Woodbridge VA
703-494-0136

Daily 10 to 10
Parking available

Quite a good selection of Mexican products here — 10 or so salsas picantes, moles (moh-lehs, not moles), canned nopalitos, and candies.   Mexican-style chorizos, cheese, and tamales.   Coffee under the labels of Cafe Tecapa, El Caporal, El Coqui, and Bustelo.   Herbs and spices such as epazote, hojas de boldo, diabetina, manrubio malvavisco.   Fresh tomatillos and Mexican-style peppers.   Votive candles and molcajetes (stone mortars and pestles).

Tienda Ebenezer

626 Grant Street
Herndon VA
703-478-0515

Monday-Friday 9 to 9 / Saturday 9 to 8 / Sunday 9 to 5
Parking available

Rosa and Fabio Ruiz have a nice, well-stocked, small store. She is from Nicaragua and Fabio is from El Salvador. They'll be able to answer questions about any of their products. Try the locally-made salteñas, or Bolivian-style meat turnovers.

Warehouse International Market

3815A South George Mason Drive
Falls Church VA
703-845-1962

Daily 9 to 8
Parking available

This store has entrances in front and in the rear, with parking in both areas. It's a popular place and well-stocked with all sorts of Latin American products, especially those from El Salvador and Peru. Here you should see quinoa, that famous Incan grain; dried potatoes and corn; frozen mangos, passion fruit, and papaya (how about a passion fruit daiquiri?); fresh fruits and vegetables; sausages; cheese; South American wines; and many canned and dried products. There's even a jewelry section.

While you're here, visit their Latin American deli at 3821D and sample some of the good-looking sweets and savories, including Bolivian salteñas and Argentine pitucas.

More Latin American Markets

Arlington Bodega
6170 Arlington Boulevard
Falls Church VA
703-532-6849

Monday-Saturday 9 to 9
Sunday 9 to 4
Parking available

Bodega Cibao
8480 Piney Branch Road
Silver Spring MD
301-588-0704

Monday-Friday 9 to 9
Saturday 9 to 10
Sunday 10 to 7
Parking available

Casa Dilone

3161 Mt. Pleasant St. NW
Washington DC
202-483-8346

Daily 10 to 10
On-street parking

Casa Latina

3702 14th Street NW
Washington DC
202-829-4998

Monday-Saturday 8:30 to 7
    Sunday 8:30 to 5
On-street parking

Casa Veiga

8709 Flower Avenue
Silver Spring MD
301-587-7747

Daily 9 a.m. to midnight
Parking available

Coqui Grocery

16248 Frederick Road
Gaithersburg MD
301-330-6798

Monday-Friday 10 to 8
    Saturday-Sunday 10 to 5
Parking available

El Gavilan

1646 Columbia Road NW
Washington DC
202-234-9260

Monday-Saturday 9 a.m. to
    10:30 p.m. / Sunday 9:30
    to 8:30
On-street parking

4301 Wilson Boulevard
Arlington VA
703-525-3822

Monday-Saturday 9 to 9
    Sunday 9 to 8
On-street parking / Near
    Ballston subway station

El Jibarito

12214 Viers Mill Road
Wheaton MD
301-929-8582

Daily 9 to 8:30
Parking available

El Mercado
7010 Commerce Street
Springfield VA
703-451-5657

Monday-Saturday 10 to 8
   Sunday 12 to 5
Parking available

El Progreso
3158 Mt. Pleasant St. NW
Washington DC
202-462-1151

Monday-Saturday 8:30 to 7
   Sunday 8:30 to 5
On-street parking

El Salvadoreño
429 South Frederick Road
Gaithersburg MD
301-948-5534

Wednesday-Monday 10 to 10
Parking available

George's
3840 Mt. Vernon Avenue
Alexandria VA
703-836-5959

Daily 9 to 9
On-street parking

El Mercado Hispano
8212 Centerville Road
Manassas Park VA
703-368-7145

Monday-Friday 10 to 8
   Saturday 9 to 8
   Sunday 9 to 7
Parking available

El Pulgarcito
7316 Carroll Avenue
Takoma Park MD
301-270-4476

Daily 8:30 a.m. to 9 p.m.
On-street parking

El Todito Market
7852 Richmond Highway
Alexandria VA
703-780-2377

Daily 9 a.m. to 10 p.m.
Parking available

La Central
85 North Glebe Road
Alexandria VA
703-528-2789

Daily 9 to 9
Parking available

La Escalerita
8640 Flower Avenue
Takoma Park MD
301-587-3589

Daily 8 a.m. to 10 p.m.
Parking available

La Tapatia
13532 Jeff Davis Highway
Woodbridge VA
703-491-8535

Monday-Saturday 10 to 8
    Sunday 10 to 7
Parking available

Los Primos
3170 Mt. Pleasant St. NW
Washington DC
202-332-8440

Daily 8 a.m. to 9 p.m.
On-street parking

Mercado Continental
4824 Boiling Brook Pkwy
Rockville MD
301-881-0333

Monday-Saturday 11 to 8
    Sunday 10 to 5
Parking available

La Preferencia
6243A Little River Turnpike
Alexandria VA

"Opening Soon" at press time

Latin American Market of Wheaton
2444B Ennalls Avenue
Wheaton MD
301-942-0503

Monday-Saturday 9:30 to 9
    Sunday 10 to 7
Public metered parking
    nearby

Mercadito Ramos
2213 14th Street NW
Washington DC
202-462-1440

Daily 9 a.m. to 10 p.m.
On-street parking

Metro Market
928 West Broad Street
Falls Church VA
703-241-8949

Daily 9 a.m. to 10 p.m.
Parking available

Mi Pais
6577 East-West Highway
Hyattsville MD
301-422-2731

Monday-Saturday 8 a.m.
   to 9 p.m. / Sunday 8 to 6
Parking available

Plaza Market
2511 Ennals Avenue
Wheaton MD
301-933-3376

Monday-Friday 9 to 8
   Saturday 9 to 7
Parking available

Tienda Diana
8519 Colesville Road
Silver Spring MD
301-565-3928

Monday-Saturday 9:30 to
   8:30 / Sunday 10 to 6
On-street parking;
Across the street from Silver
   Spring subway station

Plaza Latina Market
50 South Pickett Street
Alexandria VA
703-751-9191

Monday-Saturday 9 to 9
   Sunday 9 to 4
Parking available

Silver Spring Market
1525 University Blvd East
Hyattsville MD
301-439-8033

Monday-Saturday 9 to 8:30
   Sunday 9 to 5
Parking available

Tienda Izalco
1318 14th Street NW
Washington DC
202-232-0626

Daily 9 to 9
On-street parking

Yesenia's Latin Market

8613 Cameron Street
Silver Spring MD
301-589-0103

Monday-Saturday 9 to 9
    Sunday 9 to 6
Public metered parking
    nearby

Young's Market

Cedar Park Shopping Center
264 Cedar Lane
Vienna VA
703-849-8299

Monday-Saturday 7 a.m. to
    10 p.m. / Sunday 9 to 8
Parking available

Middle Eastern

These markets sell food products for the cuisines of the Arabic-speaking countries, Armenia, and Turkey. Middle Eastern ingredients are also sold at Afghan, Greek, Indo-Pakistani, and Persian stores.

Al Nakheel

334 Maple Avenue West
Vienna VA
703-938-4220

Monday-Friday 9:30 to 8 / Saturday 9:30 to 7
Sunday 10 to 6
Parking available

This bright, new Lebanese-owned market features a good selection of baked savories and sweets, baba ghanouj, hummous, pickles, olives, cheeses, bastirma, halal meat, and two types of frozen Lebanese sausages. There are also Middle Eastern and Persian spices, canned goods, rice, jams, pickles, and olive oils.

Aphrodite

5886 Leesburg Pike
Falls Church VA
703-931-5055

Monday-Saturday 9 to 8 / Sunday 11 to 4
Parking available

Mike and Edda Najm run one of the most interesting markets in the area and it's packed practically to the rafters with Middle Eastern and Greek food products. In early 1992, they added a fresh meat section and you can now choose from several cuts of invitingly displayed cuts of lamb and beef.

Don't pass up the excellent selections of cheeses, olives, nuts, spices, pickles, and Lebanese prepared dishes such as hummous, tabbouleh, spinach turnovers, stuffed grape leaves, and several sweets — Kayseri soujouk, bastirma, Greek loucanico sausage, halvah, jams, — the list could go on and on. Of course, it has to include the olive oils; it may take you a while to examine all the labels and firm up your choice.

Several types of bread are sold, including pita, lavash, Turkish pideh (or Greek lagana or Persian barbari), and Greek koloura. Buy some pideh, a block of Bulgarian, Greek, Turkish, or Yugoslavian feta, and some oil-cured olives. Find the nearest tree. Have a picnic.

Asadur's

5536 Randolph Road
Rockville MD
301-770-5558

Monday-Saturday 10 to 8 / Sunday 11 to 4
Parking available

Asadur's and Thomas Market (Wheaton) are now under common ownership along with Middle East Bakery (Beltsville), the pita bread makers.

Here you'll find Greek wine; canned and bulk olives; jams and preserves from Turkey and Greece; tamarind, blackberry, Jallab and Grenadine syrup from Lebanon; Greek honey; Greek hand soap; loucanico sausage; frozen green broad beans; phyllo and prepared frozen Greek dishes; frozen Egyptian mollokhia; and many kinds of nuts including pumpkin seeds, pistachios, shelled and unshelled pine nuts, roasted chickpeas, hazel nuts.

Greek coffee, dried beans, grains, fruit, cheeses, salami, soujouk, bastirma, taramasalata, olive oils, imported Turkish lokum, spices, and herbs. Breads include pita, sesame bread rings, lavash, and crusty batards.

Halal Meat Market

108 East Fairfax Street
Falls Church VA
703-532-3202

Monday-Thursday 11 to 9 / Friday 3 to 9
Saturday-Sunday 9 to 9
Parking available

In business since the late 1970's, this store is a halal meat market, grocery, and Islamic book and artifact store.

The herb and spice selection is outstanding. Bin after bin of Middle Eastern, Persian, and Indian spices provide an opportunity to experiment with new pungencies and taste sensations. There is even frankincense and, yes, myrrh.

You will also see fresh vegetables (I bought my first fresh fava beans here), fruits (including quince in season), herbs, sweet and savory baked goods, candies, bulk olives (including a low-salt oil-cured version from Turkey), fresh and frozen lamb, beef, goat, and chicken, numerous cheeses, nuts, pickles, and jams. Afghan, Indian, Persian, and Middle Eastern breads such as nan, chapati, lavash, barbari, sangak, taftoon, and pita;

The book department, now significantly expanded, houses a comprehensive selection of books on Islam in English, Urdu, Farsi, Spanish, Arabic, and Indonesian — as well as religious gifts and accoutrements.

English is spoken and everyone is quite helpful in answering questions. Plan to spend a bit of time here browsing about the shelves and reading labels.

King of Pita

6460C General Green Way
Alexandria VA
703-941-8988

Monday, Tuesday, Thursday, & Friday 9 to 5
Wednesday, Saturday, & Sunday 9 to 8
Parking available

You've probably seen King of Pita bread products all over the area. Now you know where to get them at the source, as well as quite a number of Middle Eastern grocery products.

Three sizes of pita bread are baked and sold here — from 2-inch to 12-inch — along with lavash, zaatar, sesame bread rings, turnovers, and meat pies. Baking is done daily except Wednesday and Saturday (but the grocery is still open and bread is available).

A thin pliable flat bread, lavash (or marsook) is made by stretching dough over a large round cushion until it's almost transparent. From there it's laid on an up-ended hot wok and quickly browned on both sides. It could be mistaken for a small table cloth before it's folded for packaging.

Zaatar, a pizza-like flat bread, is sprinkled with olive oil, thyme, toasted sesame seeds, and sumac (a tart Middle Eastern spice) before baking. Don't overlook the bread rings blanketed with sesame seeds — the three-cornered turnovers filled with spinach, sumac, lemon juice, and onion — and the thin meat pies topped with a tasty ground beef mixture.

The expanded grocery features typically Middle Eastern products with some emphasis on Lebanese varieties. Olive oils are imported from Greece, Spain, Turkey, Italy, Lebanon, and Tunisia. From Egypt comes frozen baby okra, kolkaz, artichoke hearts, and mollokhia. As always you'll find many Turkish canned vegetables and jams. Use the frozen falafel, made green with loads of parsley, in a delicious pita bread sandwich.

Traditional cooks will find useful the half-inch-long dried okra pods threaded on strings dangling from the ceiling — or the dried eggplant skins waiting to be softened and stuffed.

The taped Middle Eastern music may charm you into buying more than you intended.

Lebanese Butcher

113 East Annandale Road
Falls Church VA
703-533-2903

Monday-Saturday 7 a.m. to 8 p.m. / Sunday 8 to 5
Parking available

Halal meat: beef, veal, lamb, goat, chicken, stuffed chicken, chicken burgers, shish taouk (for chicken kebab), and delicious cinnamon-flavored lamb sausages made by the friendly and helpful butcher — actually there are five or so spices, but cinnamon seems to predominate.

Halloum, feta, and kashkaval cheese. Labneh made on the premises. Hummous and baba ghanouj. Olives, preserves, jams, syrups, and several canned items from Lebanon. Tahini and Lebanese coffee. Pita bread, rice, beans, wheat, fresh produce, and spices.

Lebanese Taverna Market

4400 Old Dominion Boulevard
Arlington VA
703-276-7885

Monday-Saturday 10 to 8 / Sunday 11 to 5
Parking available

At the intersection of Lee Highway and Lorcom Lane sits this new, upscale Lebanese market with eight or so cafe tables — perhaps best described as the Sutton Place Gourmet of ethnic markets. After trying some of the several prepared dishes, buy the ingredients for making your own version. Need a cookbook? They have those, too.

Hot sandwiches (shawarma, falafel, soujouk, kebabs), cold sandwiches (bastirma, hummous, baba ghanouj), salads (fattoush, tabbouleh, shakshouky), meat and cheese turnovers, stuffed grape leaves, kibbeh, and kebabs of several types.

There are fresh vegetables and fruits, including pomegranates, quince, and dandelion greens in season; bulk rice, bulgur, and beans; fresh sausage; baklavas and Lebanese cookies; and a good selection of standard Lebanese grocery items.

Mediterranean Bakery

374 South Pickett Street
Alexandria VA
703-751-1702

Monday-Saturday 9 to 8 / Sunday 10 to 6
Parking available

In spite of the 'bakery' in its name, this store, under Lebanese ownership, also has a sizeable selection of grocery products, including Armenian and Turkish coffee; Persian teas; Indian basmati rice; mashed dates for pastries; nuts; Lebanese pickles; dried Syrian apricot paste; cheeses; olives; olive oils; and many more items.

Of particular interest are the prepared dishes made on the premises: hummous, lubia bi-zeit, baba ghanouj, kibbeh, tabbouleh, pickles — and several others. Some are eaten chilled, some at room temperature, and some will need to be heated.

And, of course, don't overlook the delicious baked goods: pita bread and sweets such as baklava, mamoul, namoura, and several phyllo-based delicacies soaked in scented syrup and crowned with pistachios, walnuts, or almonds.

Mount of Olives Market

3405 Payne Street
Falls Church VA
703-379-1156

Daily 9 a.m. to 10 p.m.
Parking available

Mahmoud El-Khatib, former chef at the Saudi Arabian Embassy, runs a large operation here — a super market with a fresh meat section, catering business, bakery, and a carry-out with a couple of tables if you'd like to sit and taste. Expect to find all of the typical Middle Eastern products, including Turkish-style yogurt (which my Turkish friends say is authentic), jams and preserves, fava beans, rice, dried yogurt, and so forth. The baked savories are particularly good — meat, cheese, or spinach turnovers with all those exciting Middle Eastern herbs and spices.

Oasis Mideast Foods

1396 Chain Bridge Road
McLean VA
703-734-0326

Monday-Thursday 10 to 7:30 / Friday 10 to 8
Saturday 10 to 7 / Sunday 11 to 5
Parking available

Sparkling and new, this Lebanese market opened in the Langley Shopping Center in September, 1991. You'll find savory products such as meat "pies", kibbeh, stuffed grape leaves, baba ghanouj, hummous, tabbouleh, and stewed green beans to take out. For a sweet, choose from among several from Shatila's Bakery in Dearborn, Michigan: namoura, mamoul, baklava, and so forth.

A pleasant relief from mayonnaise-laden American potato salad is the Lebanese version with cubed potatoes sauteed in olive oil, garlic, and onions and then tossed with fresh coriander and lemon juice.

For cheese there are three types of feta (including a double-cream Egyptian version called domiati), kashkaval, Cypress haloumi, and Syrian cheese. Middle Eastern, Indian, and Persian spices are abundant as are canned goods, rice, olive oils, pickles, and chutneys.

Shemali's

3306 Wisconsin Avenue NW
Washington DC
202-686-7070

Monday-Saturday 10 to 8
Parking available

This Lebanese market features groceries, sandwiches, and prepared sweet and savory dishes for carryout. Made on the premises are tabbouleh, baba ghanouj, hummous, pickles, and baklava. Sandwiches include shawarma beef or chicken in pita bread; ground beef kebabs in pita; beef sausage with pine nuts; soujouk (similar to salami); bastirma (Lebanese pastrami); and falafel, deep-fried patties of ground chickpeas and vegetables doused in tahini sauce.

Shemali's is in the rear of the block of stores anchored by Giant Food at Newark Street and Wisconsin Avenue NW. Enter the store from the rear parking lot.

Thomas Market

2650 University Boulevard West
Wheaton MD
301-942-0839

Monday-Saturday 10 to 7
Sunday 11 to 4
Metered parking lot nearby / Near Wheaton subway station

Now under the same ownership as Asadur's in Rockville and Middle East Bakery in Beltsville, Thomas Market is one of the oldest ethnic markets in the area. After taking over in late 1990, the new owners spruced up the interior with a lower ceiling and lots of white paint.

You'll see the standard Middle Eastern products, including 10 or so kinds of olives in bulk; kasseri, kefalotiri, kefalograviera, feta, and Syrian cheeses; jams from several countries; and a good selection of nuts. For snacking, try the roasted chickpeas, either salted or unsalted — the ones that are peeled before roasting are best.

Some of the other products include Turkish and Greek halva, Greek loucanico sausage spiked with wine and orange peel, mollokhia, and Armenian cracker bread.

More Middle Eastern Markets

Baggal Market
1067 Rockville Pike
Rockville MD
301-424-5522

Monday-Thursday 11 to 7
    Friday 11 to 8 / Saturday
    9 to 4 / Sunday 9 to 1
Parking available

International Market & Deli
2010 P Street NW
Washington DC
202-293-0499

Monday-Friday 10:30 to
    midnight / Saturday-Sun-
    day 11 to midnight
On-street parking / Near
    Dupont Circle subway
    station

Georgetown Mini Market
1635 Wisconsin Avenue NW
Washington DC
202-333-1972

Monday-Saturday 9 to 8
    Sunday 10 to 6
On-street parking

Khatib Butcher Shop
3817G S. Geo. Mason Drive
Falls Church VA
703-845-9389

Daily 9:30 to 8
Parking available

Mediterranean Deli
81 North Glebe Road
Arlington VA
703-527-0423

Monday-Saturday 11 to 7
    Sunday 1 to 5:30
Parking available

Skyline Butcher Shop
3823D S. Geo. Mason Drive
Falls Church VA
703-845-5646

Monday-Saturday 9:30 to
    7:30 / Sunday 9:30 to 6
Parking available

Middle East Market
7006 Carroll Avenue
Takoma Park MD
301-270-5154

Monday-Friday 10 to 7
    Saturday-Sunday 10 to 5
Parking in nearby metered
    lots / Near Takoma Park
    subway station

Steak in a Sack
5811 Leesburg Pike
Falls Church VA
703-998-9713

Sunday-Thursday 6 a.m. to
    2 a.m. / Friday-Saturday
    6 a.m. to 3 a.m.
Parking available

Persian

Persian markets also sell Indian, Greek, Armenian, Turkish, and other Middle Eastern products.

Ali Baba Deli

1331-D Rockville Pike
Rockville MD
301-424-8888

Monday-Thursday 10 to 10 / Friday-Saturday 10 to 11
Sunday 10 to 6
Parking available

Ali Baba opened during the summer of 1992 in the new Sunshine Square strip mall. It's mainly a kebab and sandwich carryout (with three tables) and a small selection of grocery products: Persian spices, herbs, nuts, bread, several pickles (including mangos and eggplants), syrups for iced drinks, pomegranate juice, and canned dehydrated leeks, parsley, and fenugreek — ingredients for ghormeh sabsi. Try the carrot jam; it's made with carrots, sugar, rose water, and cardamom.

Assal Middle Eastern Grocery

118 Maple Avenue West
Vienna VA
703-281-2248

6039 Leesburg Pike
Falls Church VA
703-578-3232

Monday-Friday 9:30 to 8 / Saturday 10 to 8 / Sunday 11 to 6
Parking available

In these stores you will find a large selection of Persian spices and herbs; canned goods; Persian, Turkish, and Indian teas; Turkish and Armenian coffee; Persian and Turkish sweets; bastirma, a Middle Eastern pastrami; and breads, including locally-made flatbread dotted with sesame seeds (barbari), and sweet breads from California.

Flat skewers for your kebab-making are here, too.

Broad International Grocery

303 West Broad Street
Falls Church VA
703-533-2112

Daily 9 to 9
Parking available

This is the former Asia Center, which was sold by long-time owner Mohammad Ashrafi in mid-1992. The new management plans on maintaining the same type of products that have been here for several years — rice, canned goods, bread, cheese, fresh dates in season, spices, honey, dried barberries, preserves, coffee, and so forth.

Caravan

615 South Frederick Avenue
Gaithersburg MD
301-258-8380

Monday-Saturday 10 to 10 / Sunday 11 to 7
Parking available

In this typical Persian market, you will find canned vegetables from Lebanon, Turkey, and Greece; Persian breads, sweets, nuts, and herbs; Indian and Persian tea; and Turkish, Greek, French, and Bulgarian feta, along with rice, figs, raisins, dates, and olives.

Gira International

3250 Duke Street
Alexandria VA
703-370-3632

Monday-Friday 10 to 9 / Saturday 10 to 8 / Sunday 11 to 6
Parking available

Newcomers to Persian food can progress to familiarity at this combination grocery and cafe. Ezzat Sadeghi readies such tasty traditional Persian dishes as gormeh sabzi, bagheli polo, and Shirazy polo, a delicious basmati rice dish seasoned with saffron and topped with dried barberries. A recent expansion allows her to prepare kebab kubideh (ground beef), kebab-e barg (beef chunks), and joojeh kebab (chicken) over the searing flames of a charcoal grill. Accompaniments are homemade pickles, rice, and bread.

After your meal, buy a Persian cookbook and ingredients for the dish you just enjoyed. Mrs. Sadeghi is forthcoming with helpful hints.

All the typical Persian products are available — an extensive selection of herbs and spices, pickles, dried legumes and fruits, nuts, flavored waters, basmati rice, nougat (with pistachios, almonds, and rose water), sambosa and phyllo dough, and kunafa and kataifi dough threads. Breads include taftoon, barbari, lavash, and pita.

Golchin International

1110 West Broad Street
Falls Church VA
703-532-0944

Monday-Saturday 10 to 9 / Sunday 11 to 6
Parking available

Golchin opened in the spring of 1992 and features all the typical Persian products neatly arranged on immaculate shelves. Expect to find bottled syrups and juices, spices, canned tomatoes from Dubai and Iran, nuts, beans, pickles, rice, feta cheese, breads, sweets, dried barberries, and a few fresh vegetables. Perhaps one of the miniature paintings from Iran would be just the thing for your living room. Service is attentive and questions are welcome.

Gourmet International Deli

585 Grove Street
Herndon VA
703-478-6393

Monday-Saturday 11 to 7 / Sunday 12 to 5
Parking available

By the time you get to this market it may be renamed Donya Market. Donya means world in Farsi and it does seem such a nice Persian market and cafe should have a Farsi name.

This is another place to try housemade Persian food. The Vaziri brothers, Ali and Faz, will be glad to describe the dishes and what you need to buy to make them yourself. On Fridays they feature gormeh sabzi — chunks of beef simmered with spinach and beans made zesty with onions, leeks, fenugreek, and dried limes and served on a bed of saffron-flavored basmati rice. For interesting side dish try the homemade yogurt with cucumbers, mint, and rose petals.

Groceries run the gamut of Persian products, including taftoon, barbari, lavash, and pita breads; basmati rice; spices; feta cheese, olives; nuts; and fresh dates in season. They also have the flat skewers for kebab kubideh.

Rockville Gourmet
Halal Meat

1331C Rockville Pike
Rockville MD
301-424-4444

Monday-Saturday 10 to 9 / Sunday 10 to 6
Parking available

Reza Farajai brings 30 years of experience as a butcher to the Rockville area and does his own twice-weekly slaughtering in Baltimore. He opened his glistening new meat market in the summer of 1992 and is selling standard and custom cuts of halal beef, veal, lamb, and goat, along with fish and chicken at remarkably low prices. Whole lambs and goats are also available, as are the usual parts — liver, tongue, kidneys, brains, and tripe.

The only other products are several types of packaged cheese.

Villa

4801 Leland Street
Bethesda MD
301-951-0062

Monday-Thursday 10 to 8 / Friday-Saturday 10 to 9
Sunday 12 to 7
Parking available

The eat-in/carry-out delicatessen is the centerpiece here. Sandwiches include cou cou (a sort of omelette with vegetables) and Persian-style ground beef "cutlets", both served with lettuce, parsley, peppers, and pickles. Kebabs and other traditional Persian dishes are also available. Breads, spices, herbs, pickles, yogurt products, nuts, and Persian ice cream make up the grocery component.

Yekta

1488A Rockville Pike
Rockville MD
301-984-1190

Monday-Saturday 10 to 10 / Sunday 11 to 7
Parking available

Another grocery cafe, this market is one of the oldest Persian stores in the area. There is a large selection of canned goods; dried products packaged and in the bulk; olives and olive oil; Bulgarian feta; nuts; spices and herbs; Basmati and other rices; dried mulberries; Persian sweets; and Persian, Afghan and Middle Eastern breads. Fresh dates are available in season.

Jams and preserves are from Turkey, Israel, Greece, Egypt. There are kebab skewers, several Persian cookbooks in English, and samovars, tea pots, and serving glasses.

Philippine

Mabuhay Oriental Store

6615 Backlick Road
Springfield VA
703-451-8986

Monday-Saturday 9:30 to 9 / Sunday 10 to 8
Parking available

Mabuhay means welcome. Weekends are the best time to visit Sylvia and Willie Rodriguez' well-stocked store. It's then that you'll find excellent selections of such readymade Philippine staples as: bibingka, a rice flour and white cheese bun cooked in a banana leaf; pancit (noodle) dishes; roast pork (lechon); binuguan, a stew of beef intestine, pig ears, and pork blood spiked with garlic and eaten with puto, a sticky rice cake; and menudo (a stew with pork, liver, raisins, potatoes, green pepper, and seasonings). Several rice or cassava and coconut desserts are usually available. A full-fledged carryout section is planned for the end of 1992.

For those who want to sample Philippine dishes without putting it all together themselves, take a look at the large selection of mixes — including tamarind, mongo, and guava soups, and afritada, caldereta, adobo, and palabok casseroles.

Bread products by Goldilocks Bakery are sponge cake with cheese, mamon, ube roll, ensaymada, and coconut buns. Pan de sal is made in Fort Washington MD.

Nipa House Emporium

5509 Leesburg Pike
Falls Church VA
703-379-0595

Monday-Saturday 10:30 to 9:30 / Sunday to 10:30 to 8:30
Parking available

Coconut is a staple in the Philippines. So, try the coconut spread for dessert toppings, coconut jam, coconut jell and sport (young coconut) balls formed with agar-agar, and coconut sport string (long strings of coconut sport in syrup). There's an interesting gift pack, too. If you tire of coconut, look into the yam jam — a spread made from the purple-tinted tuber known as ube.

In the noodle area you'll see small packages of bean thread that are perfect for serving one person. How about some dried chrysanthemum blossoms for that next cup of tea? The package promises that "drinking (it) will bring fortune, longevity, and happiness to your family."

Instead of donuts or Danish, try the delicious ensaymada, a large, coarse-textured, and yeasted bun topped with a light coating of sugar and grated cheese — from the Goldilocks Bake Shop in California. One bun is enough for two people.

Interested in exploring further? Try the Philippine ice cream. Unfortunately it's not packaged for sampling since you'd have to fill up your trunk with half-gallons or quarts. Anyway, there's buko made from young coconut; maize; coconut sport; ube made from that purple yam and is reputed to taste a bit like blue berries; mango; golden banana with those miniature bananas with the wonderful flavor; and halo-halo filled with jackfruit, sweet beans, palm nuts, coconut sport, red beans, yam, and chickpeas — now that's a mixture!

Nipa Hut International

725 Cady Drive
Fort Washington MD
301-248-6124

Daily 10:30 to 10
Parking available

In addition to a grocery here you will find a restaurant, night club, and bakery. At Nipa Hut the market, you'll see a goodly amount of Philippine and Asian food products, utensils, cookbooks, and gift items. Look for wrappers for the famous Philippine lumpia (spring rolls), frozen lumpia, banana sauce (catsup), coconut vinegar, sausage (longaniza), taro leaves, and many noodles. In the bakery section there is a wide range of sweets and savories, including bibingka, pan de sal, ube roll, and siopao.

Philippine Fancies

739 Cady Drive
Fort Washington MD
301-248-2944

Daily 9 to 9
Parking available

Sharing a strip mall with Nipa Hut, this compact shop's atmosphere is redolent of yeast and all the other good aromas associated with Philippine baked goods. There are two styles of ensaymadas — one is a popover topped with cheese or butter and sugar while the second is similar to a Danish with coconut sport strings or cheese inside.

Rounding out the bakery selection is pan de sal, or little oblong buns. There is nothing exotic in them, but the texture is different, and they are delicious with a cup of hot chocolate or just eaten out of hand, as I did on my first tasting. The pan de leche is a small soft roll no different from your standard U.S. roll except that it seems to have a little more sugar in it. It's made with milk as the name implies.

Pan de coco is a saucer-size yeasted bun stuffed with sweetened coconut. Pan de carne is the same bun with a seasoned pork mixture substituting for the coconut. A steamed version filled with either chicken or pork is called siopao.

Hopia are biscuit-size flaky pastries filled with either sweetened yellow bean paste or seasoned pork. The six-inch Philippine cruller — or bitsu-bitso — is simply an elongated donut dipped in granulated sugar.

The shop has a good selection of Philippine groceries, including frozen fish and fruit; tocino (a sort of bacon) and longaniza (sausage); packaged mixes for casseroles, marinades, soups, and desserts; rice; canned goods; candies; and snacks.

Co-owner Myrna Maman shares her recipe for tocino with us: take a package of the frozen tocino home and put it and enough water to almost cover it in a skillet on a medium-high burner. After the water evaporates the pork will cook in its own fat until tender — takes about 45 minutes or so for the whole process.

Sampaguita Oriental Store

9205 Oxon Hill Road
Fort Washington MD
301-567-2733

Monday-Saturday 9:30 to 9 / Sunday 10 to 8
Parking available

Sampaguita, named after a Philippine flower, has all the products typical of the motherland. Introduce yourself to Philippine snack foods here:

Pili nuts, native to the Philippines and reminiscent of almonds in shape and taste, are sugar coated and roasted. As is typical of nuts, they have a high fat content, but what the heck! Chicharrones, fried pork skins, come with a small plastic dipping cup and a bag of sauce made with vinegar, garlic and hot pepper. Dried mango strips are nice and tart even though they have sugar on them.

To refresh your taste after snacking try some of the several fruit drinks; lemonade made from the calamansi fruit, a Philippine citrus, is particularly good. There are also mango, guava and soursop drinks.

Tiger Moon Market   4811 Bethesda Avenue
Bethesda MD
301-951-9180

Monday-Friday 10 to 7 / Saturday 10 to 6
On-street parking

Tess Lopez has a gem of a market and she actively caters to people who don't know too much about Philippine and other Asian cooking — witness the recipe sheets generously strewn about the displays. Pan de sal rolls with their nice chewy texture are from Laguna Bakery in Virginia Beach. Prepared foods have included bibingka, roast pork buns, spring rolls, and pad Thai. Every Saturday around noon she gives a demonstration of Philippine cooking. There is always something to taste, even if she just opens something on the spot and says, "Here, taste this; it's wonderful." And, of course, you leave with a package or two of the tasty morsels.

Ms. Lopez has created her own brand of longaniza (pork sausage), which is made for her in the Virginia suburbs. She has the traditional version with the customary amount of fat and a special lower fat version for the modern taste. Rounding out the selections are artifacts, baskets, cooking and serving utensils, and collections of typical products in gift baskets.

More Philippine Markets

C & C International
9317 Livingston Road
Fort Washington MD
301-248-9346

Monday-Saturday 11 to 9
   Sunday 11 to 6
Parking available

Oriental Food Center
5645 Annapolis Road
Bladensburg MD
301-864-7474

Open Monday-Friday 10 to
   7:30 / Saturday-Sunday 9
   to 8
Parking available

Fiesta Oriental Market
4815 North First Street
Arlington VA

Daily 10 to 8:30
Parking available

Philippine Oriental Market
3610 Lee Highway
Arlington VA
703-528-0300

Tuesday-Saturday 10 to 7
   Sunday 10 to 6
On-street parking

Portuguese

European Market

17605 Redland Road
Rockville MD
301-417-0788

Monday-Saturday 8 to 8 / Sunday 10 to 3
Parking available

Would you believe fresh fish from Portugal — sardines, pescada, garopa, chocos, carapou, shrimps with their heads still on, linguados, and salmonetes picked up in New York City every Thursday after a flight from Lisbon? These and a lot more Portuguese and Brazilian products are available here in the Redland section of Rockville.

Brothers Augusto and John Batista opened this fascinating market in December 1989, and it is truly a jewel in Washington's ethnic market crown.

You'll see loins of smoked presunto (similar to prosciutto or Westphalian ham) and several varieties of smoked pork sausage — chouriço caseiro (a country sausage with spices and wine), morcelas (blood pudding), more substantial salpicão and paio (with larger pieces of pork loin). Augusto recommends the sausages in scrambled eggs or sliced and eaten with Portuguese bread.

In the fresh meat case, you'll find beef, pork, lamb, rabbit, and free-range chicken. Some traditional items are the fresh (not cured) bacon slabs, Brazilian tasajo (a cured meat indispensable to feijoada), split salted pig feet, tiny pork ribs, and most fascinating of all, "lamb duck", a should of lamb flavored with garlic, parsley, salt and pepper and shaped to resemble a duck's torso complete with the shoulder bone forming the neck and head. This will impress your dinner guests. Roast it for an hour and a half in a 375-degree oven.

In the cheese case are queijo da Serra, a soft mild sheep's-milk cheese. With rumpled crust and soft interior it's quite spreadable. "This is the most popular cheese in Portugal," says John. Among his several other cheeses are two types of queijo saloio, queijo serrinha, and pinheiro manso.

Breads and sweets are from Teixeira's Bakery in New Jersey — pao milho (a country corn bread), wheat bread and rolls, pasteis de nata (flaky lemon custard tartlets) and amendoa (almond tartlets). At Christmas you'll see bolo rei, a beautiful, yeasted ring cake studded with candied fruits.

Among the grocery products are eight brands of Portuguese olive oil, dried figs (some stuffed with an almond or walnut), the largest raisins I've ever seen, Portuguese coffee under the Sical and Delta brands, tinned fish, frozen fava beans, pasta, mineral waters, and such bulk items as chestnuts, chickpeas, rice, and beans.

Luso Market

1022 Fillmore Street
Arlington VA
703-841-1973

Monday-Tuesday & Thursday-Saturday 10 to 7
Sunday 10-2
Parking available

This shop, near the intersection of Washington Boulevard and 10th Street, is so tiny it's almost not there. Anyway, if you can't get to European Market for your Portuguese products you may find some of them here.

Polish

Gourmet Polonez

8113 Georgia Avenue
Silver Spring MD
301-495-2650

Monday-Thursday 8:30 to 6 / Friday 8:30 to 6:30
Saturday 8:30 to 5:30
On-street parking

This downtown Silver Spring store is a bakery and delicatessen featuring Polish, Russian, and other European cured meats and canned products from Poland, Bulgaria, Russia, and Hungary.

From Poland come potato starch, pickles, dried soup, canned wild mushrooms, jams, preserves, and sauerkraut. Plum jam, rose petal jam, black currants in heavy syrup, and mustard are imported from Russia. From Bulgaria: black currant, strawberry, and apricot jams.

Sausage and meat products consist of kielbasy, kabanosy (smoked stick sausage made with beef, pork and veal), landjaeger, karaj (boneless smoked pork loin), gyulai (smoked sausage), Hungarian smoked bacon, Hungarian salami with and without paprika, Moskovskaya kielbasa (more garlic and the meat is ground more finely than in Polish kielbasa), ham sausage, blood and tongue pudding, and head cheese.

Pierogi, golumki, and pickled herring are made on the premises. A variety of cheeses is available and there is a good selection of housemade European pastries and cakes, including Greek and Polish specialties. On Fridays and Saturdays Polish doughnuts are made.

Russian

European Delight

1488-I Rockville Pike
Rockville MD
301-230-9371

Tuesday-Friday 10 to 8 / Saturday 10 to 6 / Sunday 10 to 3
Parking available

Since April 1991, owners Phil Kats and Avi Charnis have sold an interesting array of products from Russia, the Ukraine, and Poland, as well as foodstuffs made in the United States by those ethnic groups. A trip to New York once or twice a week outfits the market with tasty provisions.

You'll see smoked fish (herring, eel, turbot, trout, shad, sable, osetrina sturgeon, salmon, and paltus) and dried ribetz; caviar; canned herring and sprats, and selyodka (a Russian-style pickled herring); deli meats (moskovskaya, doktorskaya, buzhenina, medvezhya, kielbasa, Hungarian salami, lubitelskaya, zeltz yazykovi; kabanosy, and krakowska); locally-made golupki (stuffed cabbage leaves); and Russian cheeses.

Sweets include candy imported from Russia and Poland, Russian cakes and poppyseed strudels by New York's Kiev Bakery, and a tasty chocolate-covered cheese ball made by the same firm.

Frozen vareniki, blinchiki, and pelmeni comprise the dumpling department. These delights are filled with meat, cheese, potatoes, or cherries. In the refrigerator case are kefir (a yogurt drink with origins in central Asia where a fermented version is popular), ryazanka (Ukrainian yogurt), prostokvasha (Russian yogurt), Russian butter, krestyanski tvorog (farmer's cheese), and a kefir-spiked chocolate butter spread.

There are also breads, strudels (makovye pirogi), and napoleons — the best selection is on weekends; mineral waters from Georgia; kvas by the bottle or by the glass; kasha, millet, and barley; and several imported Russian canned products, including a squash paste (ikra kabachkovaya).

Don't pass up the pickled products sold by weight. There are cucumbers, mushrooms, mixed vegetables, and sauerkraut. My favorite is the outstanding whole ripe tomato ladled from a bucket of herbed and garlic-scented brine.

Look for this market behind Chesapeake Bay Seafood Restaurant. Dokan, a Persian market, is in the same strip mall.

International Food & Deli   912 East-West Highway
Takoma Park MD
301-891-1316

Monday-Friday 8 to 8 / Saturday 10 to 5 / Sunday 12 to 3
On-street parking

The brothers Mazelev from Minsk opened their carryout and grocery in March, 1992 — just off New Hampshire Avenue. It's a small shop but has an adequate selection of Russian-style food products, including sausages, dried fish, yogurt, cakes, and breads of Russian tradition. Canned goods are from Poland, Russia, and Hungary.

On one of my visits I cam away with a package of frozen cherry-filled vareniki, a crescent-shaped dumpling, and a cup of cherry sauce; a bag of frozen beef and veal pelmeni, a smaller dumpling over which you melt butter and sprinkle vinegar and black pepper; and a hefty loaf of Darnisky rye, a classic Russian rye bread made in Brooklyn.

The Mazelevs plan on offering beer and wine from Russia, Moldova, Poland, and Uzbekistan if they are successful in winning a permit from the county licensing folks.

Misha's Place of Cheese and Cheer

210 Seventh Street SE
Washington DC
202-547-5858

Monday-Saturday 9 to 7 / Sunday 10 to 5
On-street parking

Starting out as a tiny carryout offering cheese, breads, cured meats, and prepared dishes of Russia, Cheese and Cheer expanded both its kitchen and sales area in late 1991. Perhaps in response to its Eastern Market neighborhood, this market is more of an upscale gourmet store offering Russian products than a down-home Russian grocery. Weekly trips by the owner, Mikhail Vasilevsky, to the Russian community in New York yields a supply of sausages, smoked fish, "salad" dishes, knishes, and cakes. With a larger kitchen expect to find more homemade dishes than in the past. There are four or five tables available inside and on the sidewalk. Bread is from Uptown Bakers.

Thai

Asian Foods

2301 University Boulevard West
Wheaton MD
301-933-6071

Monday-Saturday 9 to 7:30 / Sunday 9 to 6:30.
Parking available

For two decades this large Thai-owned supermarket has been packed with food products, yet there's no dearth of space to move shopping carts through the aisles — a luxury that's not always available in ethnic markets. Thai products predominate, although foods of China, Vietnam, Japan, Cambodia, Indonesia, and the Philippines are in abundance.

Asian Foods has one of the largest selections of Indonesian spices, herbs, nuts, crackers and candies in the area — melinjo nut crackers, candle nuts, palm candy, kecap manis (soy sauce), several sambals (pepper sauces), kluwak nuts, ginger candy, and bumbu pecel (concentrated salad dressing with peanuts, chilis, and sugar).

Most of the frozen vegetables from Thailand don't have English translations — so you're on your own with dok sa nor, katuri, margosa, and look niang. And there's frozen turmeric root (yes, turmeric is a root before it's dried and pulverized to fit in that spice bottle) and galanga — another rhizome reminiscent of ginger with a pinkish and more translucent skin.

In the fresh meat department expect to find standard pork and fowl items, including cured duck legs and chunks of pork blood — the Chinese slice this and steam or stir-fry it. In the sausage section you'll find various types of Asian sausage including Hei Chao with cassia (closely related to cinnamon) and a liver sausage.

Then there are the Thai foods cooked on the premises for take out. Some 20 selections will probably be available on Saturdays and Sundays, with a lesser number during the week. If you don't know what to select, ask to sample some dishes. You will definitely find something that strikes your fancy.

Asian-Pacific Food Mart

7016 Commerce Street
Springfield VA
703-569-8999

Monday-Saturday 10 to 8 / Sunday 10 to 6
Parking available

Pam and Sak Prangkham, in the U.S. for some 20 years, are the owners of this shiny bright market full of intriguing products from Thailand and several other Asian countries.

Ask Pam to explain the fresh vegetables — kayaeng, a green vegetable use in Laotian curries; a kind of Laotian coriander; Laotian kaprao or holy basil; Chinese celery (mostly leaves with very little stalk); and grated long strands of green papaya for Thai salads.

At the cash register you'll see several ready-to-eat sweets and savories including sakoo, small tapioca balls stuffed with pork, peanuts and radish attractively packaged on a piece of lettuce topped with fresh coriander and a fiery little green chili. Pam also cooks kuaichop, a large flat rice "pancake" topped with boiled pork parts, boiled egg, and fresh coriander. Over this you pour the accompanying sauce.

I tried my first durian here — preserved rather than fresh or frozen. Having heard of this Thai fruit's terrible odor (but wonderful taste) I have been apprehensive about tasting it. Pam says the preservation process is merely cooking with sugar. Would this make it more palatable? The aroma was assertive but not offensive. Tastewise, the first sensation was not real positive, but after a few seconds that changed to a delightful tangy aftertaste that lingered for several minutes. Maybe I'll try the frozen version and then, when I feel like spending more money, a whole fresh one

— they weigh about 10 pounds and have large sharp spikes on the outer surface.

Perhaps more unusual are the frozen whole skinned frogs, caterpillars, and ants — or the three-inch flying insects that look like — I hate to say it — cockroaches. I understand something from the interior of the latter makes an excellent seasoning.

Duangrat Oriental Food Mart   5888 Leesburg Pike
Falls Church VA
703-578-0622

Monday-Saturday 10 to 8 / Sunday to 6
Parking available

After training in accounting in the United States, Ed Duangrat decided food would be his field. Now, he and his wife, Pookie, are the successful owner of the favorably-reviewed Duangrat Thai restaurant right behind his food market.

To get to the hundreds of Thai products, you have to dodge the big bags of rice by the door. And it turns over fast. Other than rice you're going to find the typical Thai products including frozen fish, vegetables, and fruits. There's fresh produce, too. Some Indonesian products are also available.

Everyone speaks English. Having a problem with understanding a Thai recipe? Take it here for resolution.

Sukhothai

1904 Mt. Vernon Avenue
Alexandria VA
703-683-4016

Daily 10 to 8
Parking available

A lot of products are packed into this small store, which is named after the old capital of Thailand. Buy a bottle of dipping sauce for fried chicken; it's hot and a bit sweet. Or a bag of fried pork skins accompanied by a small container of vinegar and garlic dipping sauce and the inevitable tiny green chili.

Make a special trip during the summer to buy a fresh durian, the Asian fruit described by Sukhothai staff as "tasting like heaven and smelling like hell." It's reputed to be sweet and creamy with an aroma considered rather unusual by those not accustomed to it. Cooking utensils and Thai newspapers and magazines are also sold.

Thai Market

902 Thayer Avenue
Silver Spring MD
301-495-2779

Monday-Saturday 9 to 8 / Sunday 9 to 6
Public metered parking in the rear

This long-time market (since the mid-1970's) in downtown Silver Spring just off Georgia Avenue has a sizeable Occidental clientele. Owner Dumrong Assavarungseekul and his staff are quite helpful and eager to answer your "what is this" questions. Just about everything Thai you need will be here, although they are a little light in the fresh meat department.

Standouts here are the 20 or so fish sauces (including a 2-ounce bottle for people who don't use it often); jasmine rice; frozen, pickled, and preserved fish and fish pastes from Thailand; pickled fruits and vegetables (sweet santol, mango, jujube, grapes, dyhendi, mayom, madan, guava, eggplant, plum and gooseberry); canned fruit (longan, rambutan, lychee, sapota, mangosteen, jackfruit, toddy palm seeds, sugar cane, and loquats); some 25 chili sauces; dried kaffir lime skins; dried betel nuts; jasmine rice; black glutinous rice; tum tim klob in coconut milk (an ice cream made with coconut milk, water chestnuts, and tapioca); and roasted peanuts coated with coconut milk or coffee.

One of the more fascinating items is the cold drink based on pennywort leaves. Webster says this is a creeping plant of the carrot family with crenate peltate leaves and umbellate flowers. At this point I put away my dictionary and decided just to enjoy the drink rather than know what it had in it. Or the fresh pomelo, a large citrus fruit somewhat larger than a grapefruit — in China I'm told they soak the skin in water and use the elixir to discourage ghosts and evil spirits.

Don't forget to take a look at their gifts, cooking utensils, dishes, cookbooks, and, by all means, the vast collection of video movies from Thailand — some have English sub-titles.

More Thai Markets

Bangkok '54
3832 Mount Vernon Avenue
Alexandria VA
703-549-8488

Monday-Saturday 10 to 8:30
Sunday 7:30 to 7
On-street parking

Ban Thai
8332A Richmond Highway
Alexandria VA
703-780-5031
Monday-Saturday 10 to 8
Sunday 10 to 6
Parking available

Nipa's Express Mart
208 Elden Street
Herndon VA
703-471-6278

Monday-Saturday 9 to 9
    Sunday 10 to 8
Parking available

Vietnamese

Asian Village Supermarket

2101 University Boulevard East
Hyattsville MD
301-422-3765

Monday-Saturday 9 to 9 / Sunday to 8
Parking available

Asian Village used to be Pacific Food & Gift before it was displaced by urban development on Wilson Boulevard in Arlington. The new store opened in 1990.

In refurbished supermarket quarters, this store is bright, shiny, comprehensively stocked with fresh produce, meat, fowl, and fish; frozen products including prepared dishes; canned goods; dried products; cosmetics; and other non-food products.

In response to the ethnic composition of its neighborhood, the store has many products for the cuisines of Latin America, West Indies, Africa, and other countries of the Orient.

Take a look at the fish tank from which you can select a live fish for dinner. Or choose from the 50 or so in the fresh fish department.

Eastern World Supermarket

7040 Spring Garden Drive
Springfield VA
703-569-1824

Monday-Saturday 9:30 to 8 / Sunday 9:30 to 7
Parking available

Eastern World is packed with a multiplicity of Asian food products, so much so that there's not much room in which to move about. Just say "excuse me" and squeeze by. You might find interesting the abalone-flavored soy sauce or a shrimp-flavored soy sauce from Thailand. Try the Thai nam prik pao, a concentrated seasoning of dried shrimp, garlic, onion, hot chilies, sugar, and oil.

Eden Supermarket

6763 Wilson Boulevard
Falls Church VA
703-532-4950

Monday-Friday 10 to 8 / Saturday 9:30 to 8 / Sunday 9:30 to 7
Parking available

To find this large market, look for Seven Corners' Eden Center, that varied and bustling shopping hub of just about all things Vietnamese, and you'll know you're close. Before you visit the market take a walk through Eden Center's arcade where you find several small merchants, a cafe that could easily be a replica of one in Saigon, more restaurants, a medicinal herb emporium, a music shop, a book store, jewelry stores — all in a style reminiscent of Viet Nam.

To get into the food market you'll have to go back outside. Take your time and browse among the shelves. You'll find just about any item you might need for Asian cooking, especially Vietnamese. Live carp, wonderful fresh vegetables and fruits, including sweet pea vines, lotus roots, banana blossoms, tiny hot chilies, durian, and pomelos — in season. Near the checkout area are the sweets and snacks. The brightly colored sweets, usually based on sticky rice, coconut, bananas, or sweetened bean paste, are outstanding.

Mekong Grocery

6801 Commerce Street
Springfield VA
703-644-9842

Monday-Friday 10 to 8 / Saturday-Sunday 9 to 8
Parking available

Thuong Nguyen is proud of his market's fresh meat and fowl, including the stewing chicken beloved by Vietnamese and others who like real flavor. Don't expect it to be tender in 45 minutes.

The fresh vegetables are another drawing card of this Concord Shopping Center store, along with the several cases of Chinese-style sausage (lap cheong) Thuong sells each week. Have his mainly Vietnamese and Lao customers caught on to a good thing?

My-A

11218 Georgia Avenue
Wheaton MD
301-942-6642

Monday-Saturday 10 to 8 / Sunday 10 to 7
Parking available

My-A's products are oriented toward Vietnam, however there are numerous selections from China, Taiwan, Hong Kong, and Thailand. Coconut, jackfruit, and durian ice cream from Thailand. Several pork-based Vietnamese patés. Preserved durian. Canned shark's fin soup with crab meat is a good way to try shark's fin — it's terribly expensive if you buy the fin and make the soup yourself. An interesting tidbit for your next cocktail party would be the shrimp chips — paper thin "coins" that, in hot oil, instantly puff up and make a crisp and tasty morsel with a slight shrimp taste. They are sold either colorless or in multi-hued varieties. There's no difference in the taste. Many dishes and utensils.

Saigon Imports

2927 Columbia Pike
Arlington VA
703-521-4207

Daily 10 to 8
Parking available behind the store

Here you'll find the standard Vietnamese products and a particularly good supply of fresh vegetables and herbs: Chinese celery, bitter melons, coriander, holy basil, chrysanthemum leaves, mint, lemon grass, bean sprouts, tamarinds, Asian chives, the long thin eggplants, tiny green eggplants, Asian radishes, and grated green papaya.

Thang Long International Food & Gift

8468 Centerville Road
Manassas Park VA
703-361-1421

Monday-Friday 10 to 8 / Saturday-Sunday 9 to 8
Parking available

Since late 1990 Thang Long has offered your standard Asia products with an emphasis on Vietnamese food, including the fresh vegetables and herbs favored there.

Bich chuong looks interesting: a pint jar of unshelled shrimp, sugar, fish sauce, galanga, garlic, papaya, and carrot. If you don't feel like going too far astray, try the several varieties of canned mushrooms: oyster, abalone, golden, straw, and button. The canned baby corn and, of course, rice would be useful.

Yangtze Oriental

2200 Viers Mill Road
Rockville MD
301-424-1808

Monday-Saturday 10 to 9 / Sunday to 7
Parking available

This store's Indonesian section is particularly interesting: instant ginger tea, noodle crackers, candle nuts, onion crackers, Lingham's Chilly Sauce, cassava crackers, and several Indonesian spices, pastes, seasoning mixes, and sauces (sambals).

The "crackers" are fascinating. I couldn't resist testing something whose package advised to dry the contents in the sun before frying. I assumed that wasn't necessary for the onion crackers (actually garlic crackers) since they were already about as dry as any sunshine would ever get them. They are small disks of dried tapioca flour, garlic, sugar and salt and are supposed to be fried in hot oil very briefly. I cooked mine in a microwave oven until they quickly puffed up into the size of a large thimble. Interesting stuffed with cream cheese and chopped pimentos — certainly nothing with garlic since they're already heavy with that.

More Vietnamese Markets

88 Oriental Market

6035 Leesburg Pike
Falls Church VA
703-998-8988

Monday-Saturday 10 to 9:30
Sunday 9:30 to 7
Parking available

99 Supermarket

14511Q Lee-Jackson Hwy
Chantilly VA
703-263-2769

Daily 10 to 8
Parking available

Backlick Oriental Market

6691B Backlick Road
Springfield VA
703-569-8139

Monday-Saturday 9:30 to 8
    Sunday 10:30 to 6
Parking available

Cocong Supermarket

129 E. Annandale Road
Falls Church VA
703-534-3507

Monday-Saturday 10 to 8
    Sunday 10 to 6
Parking available

Dong A Asian Market

9590 Arlington Boulevard
Fairfax VA
703-385-0430

Monday-Saturday 9:30 to
    9:30 Sunday 12:30 to 9:30
Parking available

Cantho Center

5852 Columbia Pike
Falls Church VA
703-845-5727

Daily 9 to 8
Parking available

Cu'u Long Market

3819 S. Geo. Mason Drive
Falls Church VA
703-578-1058

Daily 10 to 6
Parking available

Dong Phuong

8545 Piney Branch Road
Silver Spring MD
301-589-7970

Daily 9 to 9
Parking available

Nha Trang
7248 Arlington Boulevard
Falls Church VA
703-560-4138

Monday-Thursday 9 to 8
Friday-Sunday 9 to 9
Parking available

Vietnam Imports
922 West Broad Street
Falls Church VA
703-534-9441

Tuesday-Saturday 10 to 8
Sunday to 7
Parking available

Viet Hoa Center
7240 Arlington Boulevard
Falls Church VA
703-280-4140

Monday-Saturday 9 to 8
Sunday 9 to 7
Parking available

Vietnam Market
6613 Wilson Boulevard
Falls Church VA
703-241-0262

Monday-Saturday 10 to 7
Sunday to 6
Parking available

West Indian

West Indian markets specialize in ingredients for the cuisines of the non-Spanish-speaking Caribbean area. Markets for the Spanish-speaking countries are included in the Latin American Markets section. Most Latin American and West African markets also stock West Indian products.

Caribbean Market

11238 Triangle Lane
Wheaton MD
301-949-4423

7505 New Hampshire Avenue
Langley Park MD
301-439-5288

Tuesday-Thursday 9 to 8 / Friday-Saturday 9 to 9
Sunday 10 to 5
Parking available

In addition to their small tightly-packed Wheaton store, Caribbean Market's Guyanese owners (Rosemarie and Naraine Moonasar) now have a spacious modern Caribbean Market II in Langley Park.

Expect to see everything West Indian, including Irish moss, a vanilla-flavored drink made with Irish moss and Irish moss and stout ice cream. Just what is this Irish moss? Carrageenan, which is seaweed and is added to things to thicken them — ice cream and salad dressing, for example.

Hot pepper devotees should head for the sauce section; they'll find enough types to keep them tasting (and perspiring) for some time.

There are meats, fish, vegetables, fruits, canned and dried products. Herbs and spices include sorrel, cerasse, cinnamon leaf, chaney root, sarsaparilla, isinglass, gum arabic, arrowroot, senna leaves, eucalyptus, linseeds, and mauby bark (tastes like root beer).

Flavorings consist of vanilla, special strength vanilla, aniseed, and mixed essence (cola, vanilla, almond, aniseed, pear, lemon and lime). Fresh breadfruit and callaloo are frequently available on weekends.

Cari-Mart Foods

11325 Georgia Avenue
Wheaton MD
301-929-0096

Monday-Friday 10 to 9 / Saturday 9 to 9
Parking available / Near Wheaton subway station

Cari-Mart opened in the summer of 1991 under the management of Grace Samuels Wharwood, from Jamaica. In this pleasant, sparkling store you'll get all the help you need in selecting Caribbean products. For recipes, there are five or so cookbooks for sale. Many of the store's products are used in the entrees, side orders, and desserts on the carryout menu.

Among the selections are canned and fresh vegetables and fruits, including callaloo on weekends; frozen meat and fish (fresh fish on weekends); breads from Brown's Caribbean Bakery; spices and herbs; hot sauces; and bottled sodas.

Most of the products are from Jamaica: instant Blue Mountain coffee, chocolate sticks (cocoa, nutmeg, cinnamon, and vanilla) for making hot chocolate, an interesting selection of jams and jellies under the Caribbean Plantation label (citrus glow, a mixture of ortanique, tangerine, and grapefruit; pinepper, an explosive amalgam of pineapple and scotch bonnet peppers; mango jam; coffee jelly; and tamarind jam); and Ting, a popular grapefruit drink. In need of a tonic to clean out your system? Try a bottle of All Jamaican Roots Tonic; the label reads like a folk apothecary's dream, with 12 kinds of roots and barks mixed with honey, spices, molasses, and carbonated water.

From Grenada comes guava jelly and jam, jelly, and syrup based on the nutmeg. Lottie's Pepper Wine — sherry made lively with hot peppers — is a Barbadian concoction.

Red Apple Market

7645 New Hampshire Avenue
Langley Park MD
301-434-1810

Monday-Saturday 9 to 9 / Sunday 9 to 7
Parking available

This is the Washington area's largest West Indian market. Expect to find extensive selections, including fresh breadfruit and callaloo flown in from the Caribbean. Tubers (dasheen, cassava, malanga, coco yam, nyame). Fresh fruits and vegetables (calabaza, cho-cho, plantains). Non-alcoholic beverages (Malta India, Inca Cola, ginger beer, and other tropical colas and juices). An extensive selection of spices and herbs. Fresh fish and meat (pig's tails, cow's feet, cow's cod, oxtail, pig's feet), dried fish, self-service pickled pig's tails and snouts from small barrels, pickled fish, dried fish in brine. Frozen banana leaves and bitter gourd leaves from Philippines. Frozen jocote from Guatemala. Cassava bread from the Dominican Republic and Jamaican bread from Brown's Caribbean Bakery in Washington.

Tropical Market Place

85 Kettering Drive
Upper Marlboro MD
301-808-5306

Monday-Thursday 10 to 8 / Friday-Saturday 10 to 9
Sunday 12 to 4
Parking available

Denise Thompson, from Guyana, and her partners, Judy Grant from Jamaica and Samuel Anyang-Kusi from Ghana, opened this gleaming shopping-center market in the fall of 1991. "A taste of the tropics right in your neighborhood," said their grand opening flyer and it truly is. The store carries fresh meats, vegetables, fruits; canned vegetables; refreshment syrups; lots of herbs and spices; cheese; snacks; breads; and mixes. Don't know what something is or how it is used? Ask! Ms. Thompson, or whoever is on duty when you're there, will be eager to help.

From Grenada comes guava jelly, nutmeg jelly and jam, and a frozen savory called "crab back," or stuffed crab — a crab with the meat put back. Several products come from Jamaica, including burnt sugar (for your Christmas black cake), and cheddar cheese. Solomon Gundy, a spicy smoked fish spread, comes from Trinidad — delicious on a cracker.

Expect to find fresh vegetables and fruits, highlighted by breadfruit, callaloo, goldenapple, dasheen, and several types of yams (with the best selections on the weekend). Three kinds of bread are sold: Jamaican from Brown's Caribbean Bakery, Sybil's Guyanese bread from New York, and Effie's West African bread from suburban Virginia. Patties are Jamaican- and Guyanese-style. Ice cream in Caribbean flavors are from York Castle Ice Cream in Silver Spring.

More West Indian Markets

Coronation Market
5422 Third Street NW
Washington DC
202-723-9636

Monday-Thursday 10 to 8:30
    Friday 10 to 9
    Saturday 9 to 10
    Sunday 10 to 2
On-street parking

Kamla's Variety
5327 Georgia Avenue NW
Washington DC
202-726-0814

Monday-Saturday 10:30 to 7
On-street parking

Inter-Continental Imports
7847 Eastern Avenue
Silver Spring MD
301-589-0333

Monday-Saturday 8 to 7:30
On-street parking

Index

City Listing

ARLINGTON VA
Arlington Groc & Halal Meat (Indian) 38
Arlington Korea House 63
Asian Grocery Market (Cambodian) 12
Crescet Groc & Halal (Indian) 39
El Chaparral Meat Mkt (Latin American) 71
El Gavilan (Latin American) 75
Fiesta Oriental Market (Philippine) 104
Heidelberg Pastry Shoppe (German) 28
I. G. Int'l Foods (Indian) 40
Indian Spices & Appliances 35
International Bazar (Indian) 41
International Store (Indian) 42
Italian Store 52
Khyber Halal Market (Indian) 42
Lebanese Taverna Market (Middle Eastern) 85
Luso Market (Portuguese) 106
Mediterranean Deli (Middle Eastern) 91
Oriental Super Food (Cambodian) 12
Oriental Super Market (Cambodian) 13
Philippine Oriental Market 104
Saigon Imports (Vietnamese) 122
Sharieff Halal Meat Mkt (Indian) 44
Usman Halal Meat (Indian) 44

ASHTON MD
Wine, Beer, & German Stuff Deli 28

BELTSVILLE MD
Surya Sweets & Spices (Indian) 44

BETHESDA MD
Taiwan Grocery (Chinese) 21
Tiger Moon Market (Philippine) 103
Vace (Italian) 53
Villa (Persian) 97

FORESTVILLE MD

FT. WASHINGTON MD

GAITHERSBURG MD

Asian Food Market (Korean) 63
Caravan (Persian) 95
Coqui Grocery (Latin American) 75
El Salvadoreno (Latin American) 76
India Bazaar 40
Vace (Italian) 53

GREAT FALLS VA

Le Grand Appetit (German) 29

GREENBELT MD

Dana Bazar (Indian) 39

HERNDON VA

Gourmet Int'l Deli (Persian) 96
Indo-Pak Spices 36
Nipa's Express Mart (Thai) 118
Pooja Spices (Indian) 43
The Deli (Italian) 50
Tienda Ebenezer (Latin American) 73

HYATTSVILLE MD

Al-Mac Food Imports (African) 8
Americana Grocery (Latin American) 69
Asian Village Supermarket (Vietnamese) 119
Marinelli's (Italian) 52
Mi Pais (Latin American) 78
New York Dana Bazar (Indian) 42
Oyingbo African Market 8
Silver Spring Market (Latin American) 78

LANDOVER HILLS MD

Eko Food Store (African) 5
Express Food & Appliances (Indian) 40

LANGLEY PARK MD

Bismillah Halal Meat Market (Indian) 33

SEVERN MD

SILVER SPRING MD

WHEATON MD

WOODBRIDGE VA